Operating Systems

Operating Systems

John O'Gorman

First published 2000 by
MACMILLAN PRESS LTD
Houndmills, Basingstoke, Hampshire RG21 6XS
and London
Companies and representatives throughout the world

ISBN 0-333-80288-8 paperback

A catalogue record for this book is available from the British Library.

This book is printed on paper suitable for recycling and made from fully managed and sustained forest sources.

10   9   8   7   6   5   4   3   2   1
09 08 07 06 05 04 03 02 01 00

Typeset by Ian Kingston Editorial Services, Nottingham, UK
Printed in Great Britain by Antony Rowe Ltd, Chippenham, Wiltshire

Contents

Chapter 4 Memory manager

Chapter 5 Input and output

Preface

There are many excellent textbooks available on operating systems. While they take different approaches to the subject, they all have some features in common. Most are large books, up to 700 pages in length, and priced in proportion, aimed at students taking operating systems modules in specialist computer science courses, or computer science majors in general science courses, or even postgraduate students.

But apart from these, operating systems are also taught in a large number of other courses, although in nothing like the same detail. Almost every certificate or diploma course that has anything to do with computing contains a module on operating systems.

Students on such courses are unlikely to buy large, costly textbooks, containing more material than is required for short modules. Consequently, there is a discrepancy between what is being offered by publishers, and what is needed in the academic market.

This book is intended to fill that gap, as a text for a one term or one semester introductory course on operating systems. It contains material for roughly 25–30 lectures. The main feature which distinguishes it from other books on the market is its size. Students should, in their short course, make use of all of it, and so feel they are getting their money's worth.

Approach to the subject
Apart from the size of the book, there is also the question of the approach taken to the subject. An operating system can be understood as including everything that comes on the distribution disk. Items such as libraries, a GUI, command shells, and utility programs are frequently considered to be part of the operating system. Many books on operating systems have this underlying view, and they study them from the outside, looking at such matters as system management, use of a GUI, shell programming.

An operating system can also be taken to mean just the kernel. This is the view taken in this book. So the approach it takes is an investigation of the internals of operating systems, of how they are designed and built. There is nothing here about GUIs or shells.

The interface to the kernel is the set of system services provided by the particular operating system. There is a passing reference to the POSIX interface in relevant places throughout the text. As more and more operating systems are now providing a POSIX compliant interface, this seems reasonable.

Features

In common with other books in the Grassroots series, this text has the following features:

▶ Chapter objectives, which clearly define what students should learn in each chapter

▶ Chapter summaries, for quick revision

▶ References to further reading in a small set of classic textbooks, for those who want more information

▶ Self-test questions at the end of each chapter, so that students can assess whether they have achieved the objectives of the chapter

▶ Discussion questions, which take students into areas beyond those covered in the book.

Omissions

One feature which is commonly found in larger textbooks is an introduction to real operating systems, such as Windows NT or Unix, either as running examples, or as appended case studies. Such examples are not included in this book, because of the size of this book and their availability elsewhere. This book aims at presenting as much of the basic theory as is possible in a short course. A longer, or more intensive, course would be better served by one of the larger textbooks.

There are no quantitative examples given in areas such as scheduling, memory management, or input/output, as some textbooks do. This is not to play down their importance; the omission is due both to the size of the book and to the intended audience.

For the same reason, there are no examples of system programming in the text. While the POSIX interface is mentioned, this text does not set out to teach system programming. References to textbooks on POSIX programming are included in each chapter.

Required background

This book is not for an absolute beginner. It is assumed that a student would already have some knowledge of how a computer system works, i.e. have completed a module in computer organisation, or computer architecture, or an introduction to computing. In places, an elementary knowledge of programming is assumed, while Chapter 7 (Distributed systems) assumes an introductory knowledge of networks.

Further reading

While this text covers all of the fundamentals, because of its size this coverage is necessarily limited. It does, however, provide pointers to other material. Students taking the sort of short course that this is intended for are unlikely to get around to very extensive reading. Consequently it does not provide exhaustive references to the secondary, and even less the primary, literature in the subject.

A reference collection of about ten volumes is assumed. Between them they contain all of the background reading that might ever be needed for such a course. It is expected that all of these would be available to a student, either in a reference collection or on short-term loan. For anybody who wishes to go even further into a particular topic, the reading lists in these books will provide anything they desire.

Overview

The arrangement of the material is traditional. Chapter 1 introduces the reader to operating systems, and gives an overview of the rest of the book. Chapter 2 covers the traditional material on processes, but with more emphasis than usual on threads. Chapter 3 considers interactions between concurrent threads, including semaphores, message queues, and monitors. On the assumption that this is the only place where a student will meet concurrency, it goes into the topic in some detail. Memory management is covered in Chapter 4, including segmentation and paging. Input/output is dealt with over two chapters: Chapter 5 concentrates on the high-level device-independent aspects, while Chapter 6 looks at low-level aspects such as the interface with the hardware, control of devices, and file organisation on disk. Chapter 7 introduces the reader to distributed computer systems, and goes into some detail on communication mechanisms, and various distributed services which can be built on top of these. Finally, Chapter 8 looks briefly at fault handling and security issues, in both stand-alone and distributed systems.

John O'Gorman

Introduction

CHAPTER OVERVIEW

This chapter aims to introduce you to operating systems, and give an overview of the material which will be covered in the remainder of the book.
   After reading this chapter, you should understand:

▶ where an operating system fits into a computer system, and what it does

▶ the different interfaces to an operating system

▶ why a student of computing needs to know about operating systems

▶ how different types of operating systems have developed

▶ the main modules which go to make up an operating system

1.1   What is an operating system?

An operating system is the most fundamental piece of software running on any computer. Figure 1.1 shows in a very simplified way the basic components of a computer system. But while simple, it is important for understanding just where an operating system fits in.
   Everybody has been a user. All have used a word processor, a spreadsheet, maybe even an accounting package. These are all application programs. Figure 1.1 shows the application program interacting with the operating system.
   Now the operating system is itself a program, which is written, compiled, tested and debugged just like any other program. This program is run whenever a computer is switched on. It is almost always done automatically – no special command is required – so users may not be

Figure 1.1 Overview of a computer system

```
                    User
                     ⇕
            Application program
                     ⇕
             Operating system
                     ⇕
                  Hardware
```

aware that it happens every time they switch on a machine. It stays running all the time until the machine is switched off.

> Operating systems have been given a high profile lately. Both OS/2 and Microsoft Windows have been advertised on prime time television. But while the term is now in common use, not many understand exactly what an operating system is, and certainly not how it works.
> This book sets out to remedy that lack.

But that still leaves the question: why do we need it?

A 'raw' machine, bare hardware, is very inhospitable. It needs programming in its own binary machine code. Remember – we are dealing with digital computers. Everything is represented by numbers. English text, pictures, programs, whether in C or assembler – all are represented in the machine by numbers in binary format. Programming at this level is definitely not user-friendly.

Very simply, operating systems were invented to take some of the pain out of dealing with the raw hardware. This leads us on neatly to a discussion of what they do.

1.2 What does an operating system do?

An operating system has been likened to a government. It does no productive work itself, but provides an environment which helps others to do productive work.

So an operating system helps a user to develop and run programs, by providing a convenient environment. In the jargon that has come into use, it provides a virtual machine in place of the real machine. It does this by supplying simple functions that carry out the most commonly required operations, particularly in the following areas:

▶ Starting and stopping programs, and sharing the CPU between them.

▶ Managing memory. This involves keeping track of which parts of memory are in use and which are free. It also keeps track of which programs the memory in use has been allocated to, and provides mechanisms by which programs can ask for more memory or give back memory they no longer need.

▶ Input and output. Operating systems cover up the differences between alternative makes and models of devices. For example, the dozens of different makes and models of PC all run the Windows operating system. So all application programs run on any of them, despite the fact that no two machines are the same. In fact, when a program will not run on a particular machine, it is almost always because the programmer jumped over the operating system and contacted the hardware directly. Programmers do this sometimes to make things run faster (e.g. games), but at the cost of compatibility.

Referring to Figure 1.1 again, the operating system can be slightly different at the bottom, to suit different hardware, but must be strictly identical on all machines at the top.

▶ Another service that operating systems provide in this area is the techniques to overlap input and output with processing. While one program is taking input from the keyboard, another can be writing to a file, while a third is doing some processing. This means that the overall efficiency of the machine is improved.

▶ File systems. Every computer user takes filing systems for granted. Information is saved in a file. It can be a word processor document, a program, a spreadsheet – the user thinks up a name for it, and it is saved somewhere. Next time it is required, as long as the name can be remembered, that data is there ready for use, just as it was left. All of that work is done by the operating system.

▶ Protection. It is common nowadays to have many different programs running on the one machine at the same time, whether for different users, or for just one user. As there is only one memory, and one CPU, it is easy for them to interfere with one another. The operating system sees to it that each separate program is protected from all the others.

▶ Networking. The operating system covers up the differences between machines, so that any model of computer can communicate seamlessly with any other.

▶ Error handling and recovery. What can go wrong will go wrong. The operating system must be able to detect errors, and either recover from them or warn the user.

Finally, it is important that the operating system does all of this efficiently and economically. Resource use by the system, in terms of CPU time, memory and use of the disk, must be reasonable.

1.3 Interfaces to operating systems

The discussion so far could be summed up thus: an operating system is software which makes the hardware more useful and more user-friendly. This description may not sit comfortably with many people who have been using operating systems such as Microsoft Windows or Unix. It is not what they have known. The first thing that strikes people about Windows would probably be 'icons you click on'. A Unix user might say 'a prompt, at which you type a command'.

Figure 1.2 presents a slightly different version of the diagram.

There are two common applications with which computer users are very familiar: graphical user interfaces (abbreviated to GUI), such as Windows; and command interpreters, such as one of the Unix shells.

To see where all of these fit in, it is essential to understand that they are all only *applications*. They sit on top of, and use, the operating system, just like any other application, just like any other user-written program. They are not strictly part of the operating system but, they always come

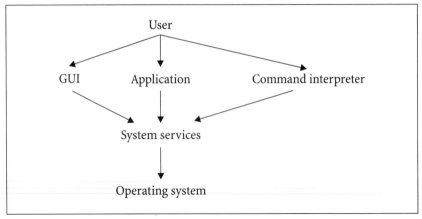

with it, and it would not be as useful without them. Just as the operating system makes the hardware more user-friendly, so these make the operating system itself more user-friendly.

Any particular operating system can have more than one of these interfaces. Nowadays it is common to provide both a GUI and a command interpreter. There is no reason why one could not be written as a student project – it is only another program.

1.3.1 The system service interface

Note that in Figure 1.2 these user interfaces, indeed all application programs, call system services. These are the *real* interface to the operating system. 'System services' is the name used to describe the set of functions provided by an operating system to enable a user to request service from it.

Just like any functions you have written yourself, they are passed parameters, they perform some operations, and return a value. The difference is that these functions have been written by the operating system designers, and are available in a library for your use.

Typically there would be hundreds of these functions. As well as the more obvious ones, such as handling disks and other peripherals, there will also be services which allow values inside the operating system itself to be queried and set.

Compilers for high-level languages use these system services all the time. For example, output commands like `printf()` are translated by the C compiler to calls on the appropriate system service for the underlying operating system.

This book will be dealing with the lower half of Figure 1.2, with the operating system itself, and an introduction to system services. We will not be dealing with command interpreters, shells or GUIs.

Until very recently, each operating system had its own set of system services. This made programs which used such system services very difficult to port to another system. Consequently, attempts are currently under way to establish a standard. The main thrust of this is POSIX – the POS standing for Portable Operating System. This is being encouraged by the IEEE.

Note that POSIX is not an operating system – it is a standard for operating system designers.

The POSIX interface is now available, to a greater or lesser degree, on almost all operating systems. Unix, Windows NT, OS/2 and OpenVMS are some examples. Because POSIX is becoming a standard, we will refer to it at appropriate places, but we are not really dealing with system programming in this book – the interested reader is referred to the reading list.

1.3.2 System services from the outside

The POSIX programming interface is relatively simple. System services are all described fully in the appropriate manuals, as supplied with each operating system. These give the order, type and meaning of each parameter, as well as explaining what aspect of the function each parameter controls.

All system services are defined as C functions. This means that they return a value. This return value is not just to be discarded. System programming is different from application programming, when it can normally be seen from the screen whether the program worked correctly or not. When a system service is called, say to change some attribute of the operating system, or write to a disk, there is no visible indication of whether the operation was successful or not. The only indication is the value returned.

> The specific meaning of this value in each case is defined in the appropriate manual page. But in most cases, if the call did not work for some reason or other, the return value is -1. If the call did work, some other value is returned. This success value should be checked to see that it is correct. It is not sufficient just to check that a call did not fail. It may have succeeded, but not done what was intended.

Normally a program should not continue after a system call fails – presumably it was called for some purpose, which has not now been achieved. However, the reason why it failed is probably more important.

> Information about why a system call failed can be obtained using the C library function perror().

1.3.3 System services from the inside

The actual C library function which the application calls does very little work. It puts the parameters on the stack and then executes a special machine instruction which causes the CPU to change to kernel mode.

At this stage we need a little detour into the hardware. All modern CPUs operate in at least two different modes. In one of these, called user mode, the CPU can only execute a subset of its instructions – the more common ones, like add, subtract, load and store, etc. In the other mode, called kernel mode, the CPU can execute all of its instructions, including extra privileged instructions. These typically access special registers which control protection on the machine. Normally the machine runs in user mode. When it wants to do something special, it has to change into kernel mode.

As well as setting the CPU into kernel mode, the C function also transfers control to the appropriate place in the operating system. This executes the requested service, running in kernel mode. When finished, it uses another special machine instruction to change the mode back to user. Finally it returns control to its caller, the application program.

Figure 1.3 shows that no matter which system service the user calls, they all pass through the one entry point into the operating system, and then go on to execute the part of the operating system code specific to each.

Figure 1.3 The single point of entry to an operating system

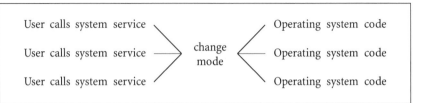

1.4 Study of operating systems

There may be a feeling at this stage that a GUI is good enough for anything we may want to do with computer operating systems – now that we have Windows, there is no need for the remainder of the book. It is certainly true that most computer users, even some computer professionals, will rarely need any more than the facilities provided by the user interface. But there are a number of very good reasons for going a little deeper than that into an operating system.

▶ There is a certain minimum knowledge of *how* an operating system does what it does that is required by anyone who is going to be seriously involved in computer systems. This is what distinguishes a professional from someone who merely uses a computer.

▶ From time to time, decisions have to be made about the selection of an operating system. To make an informed decision on this, it is necessary to understand something about the strengths and weaknesses of contending systems. This requires a knowledge not just of the terminology used by salespeople, but also of exactly what that terminology means.

▶ All operating systems are tunable. They have a large number of parameters which can affect their performance. They normally come with these set to default values. Performance can be improved by adjusting values to suit the special circumstances of a particular site. But this certainly needs some knowledge of what an operating system is doing. It is just as easy to degrade performance by making the wrong adjustments.

Many of these parameters will be met throughout the book.

▶ At some time or another, all programmers find themselves faced with a problem which the particular language they are using cannot solve. But the operating system is just waiting there, ready to be of assistance. Even if one does not study systems programming, it is important to know that there are such things as system services available, and have some idea of the sort of services they offer.

▶ Finally, operating systems are some of the largest pieces of software that have yet been written. It is an excellent exercise to analyse the structure of an operating system; to identify the sort of problems that designers are faced with; to see what options are available to solve these problems; to understand the trade-offs involved in different options; and to see which solutions were adopted – and why. In this way, the study of operating systems is largely concerned with learning the lessons of others.

Many of the ideas and techniques used by system designers are of general use over the whole field of software development. So the study of operating systems complements other courses on software design and development.

1.5 Historical development of operating systems

Operating systems did not just appear fully formed on the computer scene. As with anything else, a knowledge of where we have come from always helps in the understanding of where we are at.

Initially, in the late 1940s, there was only hardware. There was no operating system. The programmer was also the user, and in many cases the designer and builder as well. Programs and data were entered in binary by means of switches on the front of the machine. Each switch represented one bit. Output was by means of lights, with each light representing one bit. The programmer did everything that an operating system does today.

The 1950s saw the introduction of specialist operators, who were not programmers themselves, but who tended the machine, fed the programs to the machine, and delivered back the output.

The programmers no longer interacted directly with the computer. They used punch machines to encode their programs as a series of holes in stiff cards, which the computer could read and interpret. The operators acted as a *human* interface between the programmer and the hardware.

By the 1960s, human intervention was a serious source of delay in the system. Loading and unloading punched cards, starting and stopping devices – all of this slowed things down.

So instead of giving verbal commands to a human operator, the programmer punched instructions on control cards, which were inserted at the appropriate places before and after the program cards and the data cards. These commands were written in specially developed job control languages. The other side of the coin was the development of the command interface. This was a program which read, interpreted and executed the command cards. Such command interpreters are still with us today, in the form of the Unix or DOS shells. So here we have the beginning of operating systems as we now know them.

In the late 1960s we had the first attempts to provide interactive use of a computer, at a reasonable cost. The basic idea was to timeshare the computer. As the name implies, each user gets a share of the computer's time. But each user's turn comes around so fast that the system can give the impression that each one has a machine of their own. The operating system, which replaced the human operator, had to ensure that all of this worked.

In the 1970s, computer users found that programs were growing in size and required more memory than users could afford. The initial solution was to break programs up into little chunks, each of which would fit in the available memory at any one time. These were then swapped in and out as required – a time-consuming task.

Eventually operating systems came to the rescue and made memory look much larger than it really was. This virtual memory allowed larger programs to run at no extra financial cost, but it slowed machines down. So effectively we were trading speed against cost.

With timesharing, and multi-user systems of all sorts, the issue of protecting one program from another became more and more important. Once again, operating systems took on the responsibility.

One of the significant developments of the 1980s was networking. The hardware ability to link machines together led to demands on operating systems to control this communication. There was a certain fusing of the fields of operating systems and computer networks.

Networking has grown from merely connecting machines to providing shared resources such as file systems or printers. Network operating systems were developed to control this (Windows for Workgroups, Novell NetWare etc.). By the end of the 1990s things had reached a stage where groups of machines acted as one, collaborating on some task. We talk about distributed systems, and of course they call for distributed operating systems to control this sort of interaction.

Another feature of operating systems in the 1990s was the move to open systems. Previously, operating systems had been developed specifically for particular hardware platforms, e.g. MS-DOS for the PC or VMS for the VAX. Now there is a move to build generic operating systems (e.g. Linux) which will run on any hardware.

1.6 Types of operating system

From the overview given in the previous section, it is not surprising that many different types of operating system have grown up over the 50 year history of computing. This diversity is due to attempts by designers to meet particular requirements and to write specialist systems dedicated to specific purposes.

The most important distinction that has arisen historically is between *batch* and *interactive* systems. Then there is the combination of these in the *general-purpose* system. Of late, *network* and *distributed* systems have become important. There are also some very specialized systems, which we will not study. It will suffice to mention them in passing.

1.6.1 Batch systems

Historically, these were the earliest systems developed, so we will look at them first.

In such a system, the program, the data and the commands to manipulate the program and data are all submitted together to the computer in the form of a 'job'. There is little or no interaction between users and an executing program. Obviously this is not very suitable for program development, even though it was once used for this.

There is still a niche market for batch systems today. In any situation where the data is all available and there is no need for interaction with a running program, a batch system is quite adequate. One classic example of this is payroll processing, where all of the information on hours worked, rates of pay, tax allowances etc. is available beforehand, and the computer can be allowed to run on its own, printing payslips. Another example is printing account statements, such as bank or credit card statements. There is no need for any operator interaction once the job has been started.

The advantage of a batch environment is that it can provide a wide variety of different devices and software, which it would not be cost-effective for an individual user to purchase.

1.6.2 Interactive

This is the most common mode of computing today, using keyboard, mouse and screen. It is what most people think of when they say computing. For a programmer, it is a significant improvement on batch systems, as it is now possible to intervene directly while a program is being developed, or as it is running.

Single user
Some systems provide interactive computing on a single-user basis. Examples would be Windows NT and OS/2.

The present state of the art is a single-user machine which is multitasking. It does more than one thing at the same time, for the one user. The motivation behind this is to improve productivity, but it brings up the whole question of protection. One job must not have free access to files, data, or programs belonging to another. On the other hand, there may be times when you want to share data between programs – so the protection has to be selective. A significant proportion of operating system code is involved with dealing with this.

Terminology in this area is very confusing (and confused). Different companies and authors use the same words with different meanings, and different words to mean the same thing. In general, we can take *process* to mean the same as *task*, so *multiprocessing* is the same as *multitasking*. But be warned that this is not universally true. Some authors reserve multiprocessing for computers with more than one CPU.

Multi-user

Other systems provide interactive computing on a multi-access or multi-user basis. We will take that to mean simultaneous access to a computer system through two or more terminals. Unix is an example of this.

The motivation behind this is the sharing of resources and information.

1.6.3 General purpose

In practice, a given environment may want a bit of everything. For example, a timesharing system may support interactive users, but also include the ability to run programs in batch mode. So we speak of general-purpose systems.

1.6.4 Network operating systems

It is a common practice today to share resources such as printers and databases across a network. Network operating systems handle the underlying processes required for such sharing.

A further development in this area is the integration of NOS with the general-purpose operating system already found on desktop workstations. Windows NT Server is an example, and Unix can also be configured this way.

1.6.5 Distributed systems

This is the most recent development in operating systems, meeting the requirements of a multi-user system in a new way. Essentially, it consists of a group of machines acting together as one.

Thus when a user starts a program, it may actually run on the local machine. But if that computer is heavily loaded, and the operating system knows that another machine is idle, then the job may be transferred to that idle machine.

All this migration of data or of programs from one machine to another is totally under the control of the distributed operating system, and the user is not aware of it.

1.6.6 Specialist systems

Some specialized operating systems have also been developed, each with its own particular application area. For example, a real-time operating system would be used in situations such as chemical plants, life support systems, or fly-by-wire aeroplanes. Such a system guarantees that it will respond within a fixed time.

Specially designed operating systems would be in order when the computer system is dedicated to processing large volumes of data, which are maintained in an organized way. Examples would be a student record system or a library database. The operating system must hide the organisation and structure of the data from the user and optimise it for fast response to requests.

If there are frequent changes to the data, such as in airline seat reservation systems or banking systems, then we speak of transaction processing systems.

1.7 Design of operating systems

An operating system is a large – very large – piece of software. To design, build and maintain large software systems requires a high-level view of how the system is structured and how its different components work together. So we can start with a top-level break down of an operating system.

At this level of detail, an operating system can be decomposed into modules which would provide the following functions:

▶ Process management

▶ Memory management

▶ I/O management

▶ File storage, which uses I/O and adds protection and security

▶ Network management

Such an operating system is illustrated in Figure 1.4. Subsequent chapters will look at each of these modules, one by one.

Figure 1.4 Modular operating system

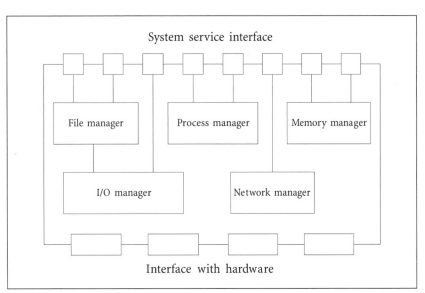

Operating systems have tended to grow larger and more complex. A relatively new proposal is to restructure the operating system into two layers. The lower layer is the microkernel, which provides the absolutely

minimum facilities. For example, at the hardware level, complicated setting and testing of bits in registers may be needed to get a character to a printer. The I/O management layer in the microkernel provides a function to do this which hides all the details of hardware, not to mention the complication of different models of hardware.

Above this microkernel is a layer which provides optional extra services, as well as emulating a particular system service interface. The microkernel provides its own private interface, which is used by any emulation layer built above it.

It could even be possible to emulate more than one system service interface at the same time. Figure 1.5 shows a microkernel with both a POSIX interface, and a Microsoft Win32 application programming interface layered above it. Sometimes these are referred to as different 'personalities'. The NT operating system is built like this.

Figure 1.5 Microkernel with two personalities

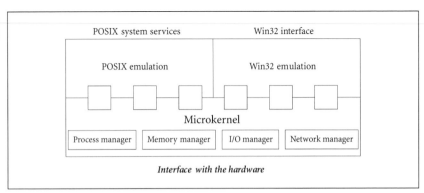

CHAPTER SUMMARY

▶ An operating system is a program which sits between the raw hardware and applications. It provides a user-friendly interface to applications programmers, hiding the complexity and diversity of the hardware.

▶ It provides an environment which makes it easier for applications programmers to do productive work. It:

– supplies simple functions that carry out the most commonly required operations

– manages and shares the resources of the computer system, such as CPU, memory, disks and printers

– hides some differences in the hardware.

It does all of this as efficiently and economically as possible.

▶ Most users are familiar with graphical user interfaces and command interpreters. These are just applications which sit on top of the operating system and make it more user-friendly. Like all applications, they in turn make use of system services. These are the real interface to an operating system.

Systems services are the functions which the operating system offers to perform on behalf of applications programs.

Internally, each system service is only a wrapper which switches the CPU into kernel mode and calls the appropriate kernel function. Afterwards it switches back to user mode and returns to the caller.

▷ A certain minimum knowledge of how an operating system does what it does is required by anyone seriously involved in computer systems. A user may be required to choose, or tune, an operating system. Many of the techniques used by system designers are relevant in the wider field of software development.

▷ The earliest computers had no operating systems, with the programmer operating directly on the hardware. The first operating systems were human operators.

In the 1960s, verbal commands to operators were replaced with machine-readable commands written in job control languages. In the late 1960s, timesharing led to operating systems taking over the scheduling of machines.

The 1970s was the era of virtual memory. Then in the 1980s, networking and the GUI were the development areas. Distributed systems and open systems were at the forefront of operating systems research in the 1990s.

▷ Many different types of operating system have been developed to meet particular requirements. The most important distinction that has arisen historically is between batch and interactive systems. In a batch system, the program and data are submitted together in the form of a 'job'.

Interactive systems are where the user is involved in a dialogue with the computer, using keyboard, mouse and screen. Some systems, such as Windows NT and OS/2, provide interactive computing on a single-user basis; others do so on a multi-user or multi-access basis.

Both of these are frequently combined in general-purpose systems. There are also specialist systems for controlling networks, and distributed operating systems for controlling groups of machines acting together as one.

▷ It is now accepted that large software systems, such as operating systems, should be designed and built in a modular fashion. The top-level decomposition of an operating system would include modules to manage processes, memory, I/O, communications and file systems.

A more recent design trend would isolate the absolutely necessary features in a microkernel. Other services can then be layered on top of this.

FURTHER READING

All books on operating systems cover this introductory material. For example, Silberschatz and Galvin Chapter 1; Nutt Sections 1.1, 3.2; Tanenbaum and Woodhull Section 1.1; Stallings Chapter 2; Tanenbaum (1992) Chapter 1. For more on the system service interface see

Silberschatz and Galvin Sections 2.6, 3.2, 3.3, 21.3; Nutt Section 3.3.3; Tanenbaum and Woodhull Sections 3.1, 3.2; Stallings Section 1.7. The historical introduction is also covered in Tanenbaum and Woodhull Section 1.2. Nutt Section 1.2 deals with the different types of operating system. Material on operating system design can be found in Silberschatz and Galvin Sections 3.1, 3.5, 3.7; Nutt Section 3.1; Tanenbaum and Woodhull Section 1.5.

SELF-TEST QUESTIONS

1 Explain where an operating system fits into a computer system.

2 List and explain the most important functions of an operating system.

3 Explain the difference between a GUI, a command interpreter and the system service interface to an operating system.

4 Outline how a programmer uses the POSIX interface to an operating system.

5 How does system service code get to change the CPU to run in kernel mode?

6 Justify why the study of operating systems is relevant to a student of computing.

7 Outline the historical development of operating systems.

8 Distinguish the different types of operating system which have developed.

9 Briefly describe the main modules which go to make up an operating system.

DISCUSSION QUESTIONS

1 An operating system is an extra layer of software in a computer, extra instructions to be executed, which slows an application program down. Discuss the advantages and disadvantages of removing operating systems altogether.

2 Many of the things an operating system does seem to be relevant to large multi-user systems – overlapping input and output, communicating with other machines and providing virtual memory. Is such an operating system really needed on a single-user personal computer?

3 Is Windows NT an operating system? Or a GUI? Or both?

4 Check the manual page for the read() system service. Describe all of the checks you would have to perform on the value returned by this function to be sure that you had covered every possibility.

5 All system services call a special machine instruction which causes the CPU to change to kernel mode. It seems that you could write your

own assembler program, using this instruction, and hence take over the machine yourself. Investigate the special instruction on the hardware you are using, and find out why it is not as easy as it seems.

6   Do you find the arguments given in Section 1.4 convincing? Why? Or do you think operating system courses should be abolished? Can you think of any other reasons why they should be part of a computer systems course?

7   Early computer systems got on without operating systems. What has changed that we need them today?

8   What might be the next big breakthrough in operating systems?

9   What use is a multitasking operating system on a single-user machine? Surely one user can only do one thing at a time?

10   Distributed systems certainly seem to have great advantages. List some aspects which might make you slow to move from standalone systems.

11   An operating system designed with either of the methods we have discussed would require significant rewriting if moved to a machine with different hardware. Discuss how an operating system might be designed to minimize this.

Process manager

In the previous chapter, the modules which go to make up an operating system were identified. This chapter aims to introduce you to the first of these, the process manager.

After reading this chapter, you should:

▶ be familiar with both the static and dynamic aspects of a process

▶ understand the relationship between processes and processors

▶ be familiar with the concept of multiple threads of control in a process

▶ understand how processes and threads are represented within an operating system

▶ understand how processes and threads are created and terminated

▶ be familiar with the life cycle of a thread

▶ understand the mechanics of context switching, and of scheduling

2.1 The concept of a process

A *process* is the unit of work in a computer system. There are two aspects to any process, a static part and a dynamic part.

The static part, which we will refer to as a *task*, involves the resources allocated to the process. This includes a certain amount of space in memory, a current working directory, sources of input and output such as a keyboard, screen and open files, and maybe a connection with another process over a network. The most important resource which any process has, though, is a program. A *program* is a sequence of instructions. On its own, a program does nothing. It is inert.

The dynamic part of a process can be described as 'a program in action'. When the instructions that make up a program are actually being carried out, the CPU works its way through the program in a particular pattern. A program typically involves branches and loops, so this pattern may be the same each time the program is run, or it may be different. This dynamic part of a process is known as a 'thread of execution', or a 'thread of control', or just a *thread*. A thread has access to all of the resources assigned to the task.

There is some similarity between an operating system process, and baking a cake. The task corresponds to the ingredients (resources), including the recipe (program). The thread is the actual sequence of operations carried out, as directed by the recipe, for example mixing, baking, and maybe even eating. The process is the whole job of work, which we might describe as 'make a cake'.

A very formal definition of a process would be 'a sequence of states, resulting from the action of a set of instructions on the states as they develop'. At first sight this does not seem to be the same thing. It seems to be a purely static concept, with no dynamic aspect at all. So it is necessary to explain what is meant by a computational state in this context. It is like a photograph of the internals of the computer, taken at a particular instant. It includes the values of the CPU registers, the values in each byte of memory and the values in each of the special registers associated with hardware devices.

At any given time, the computer is in a particular state. Then an instruction is executed. This changes at least one value somewhere in the machine, and moves it to a (very slightly) different state.

Consider the small assembler program given in Figure 2.1. Line 1 loads the value 7 into register 0. Line 2 increments the value in register 0. Line 3 stores the value from register 0 to a memory location (total).

Figure 2.1 Program to illustrate change of state

```
1:    ld #7, r0
2:    inc r0
3:    st r0, total
```

The sequence of states corresponding to the execution of this program is shown in Figure 2.2. We are only interested in the program counter (PC), one CPU register (r0) and one memory location (total). Obviously there are many other elements which go to make up the full state of the machine, but only those shown are relevant to the example.

Figure 2.2 States as program executes

	PC	r0	total
Initial state	1	0	0
State after 1st instruction	2	7	0
State after 2nd instruction	3	8	0
State after 3rd instruction	4	8	8

So the definition is saying that a process consists of all of these states, from the initial state to the final one. It is similar to a movie, which is made up of hundreds of thousands of still pictures. When we view all of them in the correct order, we have the movie.

This idea of a process as a sequence of states includes both the static task and the dynamic thread of control. It will be important when we come to consider several processes running on one machine at the same time.

2.2 Processors and processes

A *processor* is the agent which runs a process by executing the instructions contained in its associated program. Typically, there are far fewer processors than processes. In fact, in most cases there is only one processor. So processes get their share of time on the processor. This would only be when they are in a position to do some work – a process is never offered the processor while it is waiting for keyboard input, for example.

Consider the situation outlined in Figure 2.3, where the solid lines represent CPU execution and the dashed lines represent the operation of a disk drive.

Figure 2.3 Overlap of processor and devices

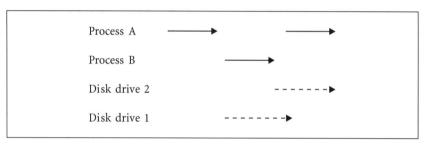

Process A is executing on the (one) processor. It sends a request to read data from drive 1. The disk drive begins the read operation, but this will take some time, as the head has to move and the correct sector has to be under the head before it can read.

In the meantime, process A cannot continue. So the operating system gives the processor to process B. This process executes some instructions, then sends a request to read data from drive 2. While waiting for this data, process B cannot execute any further instructions.

Now if these are the only two processes on the machine, the CPU is idle. Note that the two drives can be operating at the same time, as they are separate physical devices. Also, one process can be operating on the CPU while the drives are working. But there can be no overlap of processes. Only one can be active at any given time.

Eventually, drive 1 delivers the required information. The operating system copies the data from drive 1 into the memory space of process A, and restarts that process at the next instruction after the request for data. It proceeds from there.

Some time later, drive 2 delivers the information it was requested to read. At this stage, the operating system can allow process A to continue. Or, as B has been idle for quite some time, it might seem fair to give B some processor time now. The resolution of this question is left until we consider scheduling in Section 2.9.

2.3 Multi-threading

We have seen in the previous section that sometimes a process is running on the processor, building up state. At other times it is idle for one reason or another.

It happens frequently that a process begins running on a processor and almost immediately stops again to wait for some input to become available. The state of the machine has to be saved and the saved state of some other process restored. This is no sooner done than that process in turn stops, and all this saving and restoring has to be done again. Remember: saving and restoring state is non-productive work, and here it is becoming a large part of the overall work of the computer.

> The overhead involved in moving from running to idle, or vice versa, can be considerable. The operating system has to save the whole state of the machine as it was at the moment when the process stopped running. There is a similar overhead involved when a process begins running again. All of the saved state has to be restored and the machine set up exactly as it was when the process last ran. And this overhead is on the increase as the number and size of CPU registers grows and as operating systems become more complex, so requiring ever more state to be remembered.

This has led to the idea of having a number of paths of execution (threads) through the program at the same time. With such an arrangement, if one thread is blocked another can execute. It is not necessary to save and restore the full state of the machine for this, as it is using the same memory, files and devices – it is just jumping to another location in the program code. But each thread must maintain some state information of its own, for example the program counter, stack pointer and general-purpose registers. This is so that when it regains control it may continue from the point it was at before it lost control.

So now a task can be viewed as an environment in which one or more threads can execute. A standard process consists of a task with a single thread; but processes may have more than one thread.

> The example we used earlier, of baking a cake, can be extended to baking several cakes. We still have only one process. There is one task, or set of resources, though there may be more of them. There is only one recipe. But while one cake is in the oven, we may be mixing the ingredients for another. We are following the recipe at two different places at the same time. Instead of idly waiting for the first cake to be baked, we are using that time productively.

2.3.1 Example

A file server is a good example of the usefulness of multi-threading. If there is only one thread, then it can only handle one request at a time. As it will spend quite a proportion of its time waiting for the disk drive, the total amount of work it does for its clients will be nothing near its capacity. Figure 2.4 illustrates this under-use of resources. The CPU is idle some of the time, and drive 2 is idle all of the time.

Figure 2.4 An underutilized system

However, if there are many threads of control in the server process, while some are blocked waiting for the disk drive, another can be processing a request from a new client. In this way the server is limited only by the capacity of the disk drive to provide information. Figure 2.5 illustrates this situation, with the CPU fully occupied and both disk drives in fairly constant use.

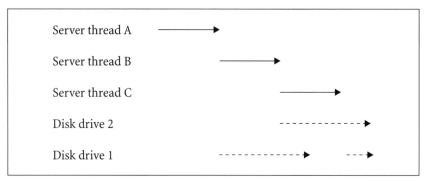

Figure 2.5 High utilisation of CPU and disk drives

2.3.2 Implementation

Sometimes a threads package is implemented as a set of library routines running entirely at user level. This saves on the overhead of bothering the operating system each time control changes from one thread to another. The operating system gives control of the CPU to a process. The program that the process is executing calls library functions which divide up its time among a number of threads. This approach has the serious drawback that if one thread calls a system service such as `read()` and it blocks, waiting for a key to be pressed, the operating system will block the whole process and give the CPU to another. It just does not know about threads. It might be viewed as a cheap way to implement threads on top of an existing system.

The other possibility is for threads to be implemented in the operating system itself, which then handles all the switching between threads. This allows multi-threading to be used to full advantage.

2.4 Representing processes, tasks and threads

The operating system needs to keep track of processes. As with all software systems, it uses data structures to represent the different objects it is dealing with.

For each process that is currently known to it, the operating system maintains a data structure known as a process descriptor or a process control block. Such data structures can be implemented statically in fixed size tables. This has the advantage that the information relating to a particular process can be found immediately by indexing into this table. The downside is that there can be quite a lot of wasted space, for example if there are only a few processes running and space has been allocated for hundreds. On the other hand, there is a maximum number of processes that can be running at one time.

Another possibility is to allocate space dynamically, as required, and only for as long as required, usually as a linked list. This means that there is never too much or too little space allocated for process control blocks. The drawback is that you cannot index into such a linked list – you have to search it sequentially to find a particular process. This has to be done very frequently, so it represents a very large overhead.

When we come to examine this data structure representing a process in detail, remember that we have distinguished between a task, which is the resources allocated, and one or more threads, or control paths, through the code. So the process data structure cannot be 'one size fits all'. It must be possible to represent the one task and a variable number of threads. It needs a static part, and a dynamic part that can grow or shrink. This is implemented by means of a linked list, as illustrated in Figure 2.6.

Figure 2.6 Linked list of data structures to represent a process

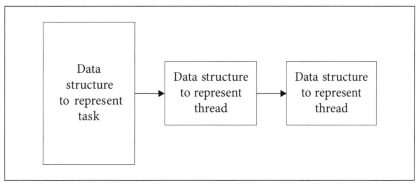

2.4.1 Task

Let us begin with the static part, which is the same for all processes. Figure 2.7 illustrates some of the fields which might be present in this `task` structure.

It identifies the owner of the process. The operating system uses this information to determine whether or not to grant a process access to

Figure 2.7 Data structure representing a task

owner
unique process id
address space description
program starting address
data starting address
stack starting address
list of threads
number of threads
open file information
default directory

specific system resources. Each process is also given its own unique process identification number (pid) when it is created.

The task structure may also contain information about the memory used by the process, including the addresses of where the program code, the data, and the stack, are in memory.

There will be a header of the list of threads associated with this task, as well as a count of the number of threads. There will be information about the sources of input and output which the process has open, as well as a note of its default directory.

A realistic `task` structure would have many more fields than this. What we have shown here will give a flavour of the sort of information which has to be recorded about the static part of each process.

2.4.2 Thread

The kernel also maintains a `thread` data structure for each active thread (see Figure 2.8). Many of the fields in this structure will only become relevant later on in this chapter. For the moment, we can understand the first two, a pointer back to the `task`, and a pointer to any further `thread` structures.

One of the more important fields in this `thread` structure is the volatile environment (see Figure 2.9). This has fields for the information

Figure 2.8 Data structure representing a thread

task to which I belong
list of threads in task
volatile environment
state
links
thread's base priority
maximum priority
current priority

Figure 2.9 The volatile environment of a thread

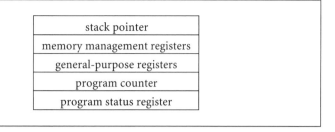

that has to be saved each time the thread loses control of the CPU. As you can see, it consists of copies of the values in the CPU registers, a sort of snapshot of the state of the CPU at the moment the thread stopped executing.

2.5 Process creation and termination

All operating systems have some way of creating new processes. A process control block representing the new process is created and added to the others already there. It then competes with them for a share of CPU time.

In POSIX the system service which creates a new process is fork(). This creates an exact copy of the running process. So immediately after the call to fork() there are two processes, each executing the same program. Each of them is at exactly the same point in the program – the next instruction after the fork() – and both will continue on from there.

The three line example in Figure 2.10 illustrates this.

Figure 2.10 Program to illustrate fork()

```
printf ("Before the fork\n");
fork ();
printf ("After the fork\n");
```

Before running this program, work out what output would be expected on the screen and why. Then try the program. Were the results as expected? Normally the duplication of the second message would be considered an error. After all, the program was only told to print it once. But of course after the fork(), there are two copies of the program running, and each prints the message once.

This is not very useful. Normally, one of them then asks the operating system to run another program, so the end result is one process executing one program and the second process executing the other.

The child process created by fork() has only one thread, a clone of the one that called it.

> Some operating system interfaces provide a system service which both creates a new process and runs a new program in that process. In this case, the name of the program to be run must be a parameter to the system service.

A process terminates when the program it is running comes to an end. Alternatively, it can call the exit() system service anywhere in its code. This lets its parent know that it has finished, and it can also pass back some information about why it finished – whether this was normal or abnormal.

2.6 Thread creation and termination

We have seen that a new process begins life with only one thread of control. But it is possible to create other threads within the process after it has begun to execute. A new thread structure is created and added to the linked list.

One interface used for creating, manipulating and terminating threads is the POSIX pthread library of functions, which we will describe here.

2.6.1 Thread creation

A new thread is created by calling the pthread_create() function. One parameter to this specifies where the new thread will begin execution. As the new thread belongs to the same process, it must execute code from within the same program. But it cannot start just anywhere. Each thread starts at the beginning of some function, known as its start routine.

Remember that you are not calling the function – you are passing its address to the thread creator. The difference between calling a function, and creating a thread to execute a function is illustrated in the upper and lower parts of Figure 2.11. With a function call, execution of the main program is suspended until the function has completed; it then resumes at the instruction after the function call. When a new thread is created to execute a function the main program is not held up; both continue in parallel.

Figure 2.11 Function call and thread creation

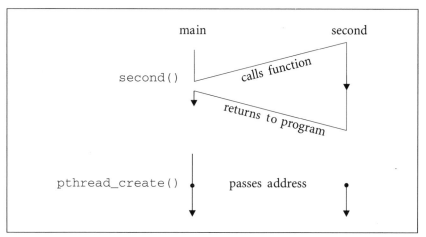

If you run low on flour while baking, you can stop what you are doing and go to the shop to buy some more. Then, when you return, you can take up exactly from where you stopped. The other possibility is that you can send someone else to the shop (in good time), while you continue with what you have.

Each thread has its own stack, so it can have its own private copy of local variables. Another thread executing the same function will have a different copy of these variables. That is why the stack pointer is saved as part of the volatile environment.

2.6.2 Thread termination

A thread stops executing when it comes to the end of its start routine. Alternatively, a thread can call `pthread_exit()` anywhere in its code. But in all cases the data structure representing the thread remains in the system. It is finally removed when some other thread calls `pthread_detach()`.

2.7 Thread state

Each thread has a life cycle of its own, during which it may be in one of two different states. The state a thread is in at any particular time is recorded in the `state` field of the `thread` structure.

It may be in the RUN state. This means that it is ready and able to do some work. Typically there would be many threads in this state, linked together on a run queue. But on a single-processor machine only one thread can be using the CPU at any one time. On a multiprocessor, of course, as many threads as there are CPUs can be actually executing.

A thread may be in the WAIT state. This means that for some reason or other it is unable to use the CPU, even if offered it. In general, a thread in this state is waiting for some event. This may be a physical resource, such as a printer or a modem, or it may be waiting for an event such as a key to be pressed, or (as in Section 2.2) waiting for requested data to be delivered from a disk. Threads in the WAIT state are linked together on a wait queue.

In either case, the `thread` structure is maintained on the appropriate queue through the `links` field.

The possible transitions between the states are shown in Figure 2.12, which, for completeness, also shows where threads enter and leave the system.

Figure 2.12 Thread states and transitions

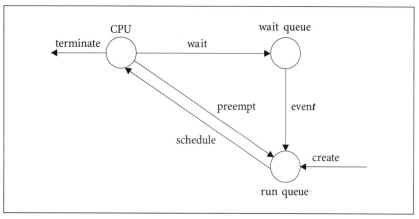

25

When a new thread is created, it always begins in the RUN state on the run queue. Eventually it will be given a time slice on the CPU. When this transition takes place is the responsibility of the scheduler.

A thread may stop using the CPU for three reasons. It may do so voluntarily, while it is waiting for a resource, in which case it moves to the WAIT state. It may decide to terminate itself or the whole process. Or the operating system may take the processor from it, even though it has further instructions to execute. This is called preemption. The operating system does this when a thread has used up its share of time, or when the CPU is needed to handle some more urgent work. In either case, when a thread is preempted it moves back to the run queue.

A thread leaves the WAIT state when the event it is waiting for occurs. The only way it can move is to the RUN state, where it will take its turn and eventually move back to the CPU.

2.8 Context switching

This is the name given to the whole procedure of reallocating a processor from one thread to another. As we have seen in the last section, apart from terminating, a thread loses control of the processor for one of two reasons. Either it moves into the WAIT state to wait for a resource to become available, or a timer interrupts to tell it that it has used up its time slice. In both cases the context switcher is called.

It is absolutely essential that the current state of the machine be saved when a thread loses control of the CPU. This state includes the values in the general-purpose registers, stack pointer, memory management registers, and most especially the processor status register and the program counter. When, at some time in the future, the thread now being switched out becomes eligible to run again, it will then be possible to set up the machine exactly as it was after the last instruction was executed. So the next instruction will operate on the correct state, and the thread (sequence of states) will continue properly.

This state, or volatile environment as it is sometimes called, is saved in the thread structure of its own thread. Presumably the state of the new thread to be run is available in its thread structure. It was saved there when it was context-switched out some time previously. This state is now copied from the volatile environment field to the appropriate registers.

The order in which the various items of information are copied from the thread structure to the registers is not important, except that it is essential that the value of the PC be the last item moved. Remember that there must be some program giving instructions for all of this moving. It is in fact the context switcher. While it is running, the PC is pointing to context switcher code. If the PC were the first register restored, then the next instruction would not be taken from context switcher code, but from wherever the PC is now pointing – into the middle of the new program. So that program would be started up without all of its state. This would lead to chaos.

The sequence of operations involved in context switching is shown in Figure 2.13, with time running down the page.

Figure 2.13 Context switching

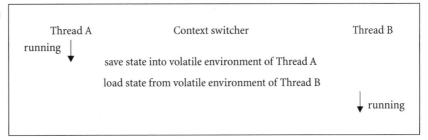

2.9 Scheduling

The previous section examined how a thread is given a chance to run on a processor. Scheduling determines *which* thread will be next.

The main objective of the scheduler is to see that the CPU is shared among all contending threads as fairly as possible. But fairness can mean different things in different situations. In an interactive system, the scheduler tries to make the *response time* as short as possible. A typical target would be 50–150 ms. Users can find it quite off-putting if the response time varies wildly, say from 10–1000 ms. If one keystroke is echoed immediately, and the next is not echoed for a second, a user is inclined to press the key again, with all the consequent errors.

A batch system will not be concerned with response time but with maximising the use of expensive peripherals. Many different scheduling algorithms have been developed for such systems.

In real-time systems, the scheduler will have to be able to guarantee that response time will never exceed a certain maximum. For example, a multimedia system handling video and audio must have access to the processor at predefined intervals.

> One very simple scheduling arrangement would be static fixed ordering. This would be suitable in a process control situation. The function and duration of all threads would be known in advance at design time. So a decision can be made once and for all on who goes next.
>
> For example, a thread controlling a sensor may be run, followed by a thread which does some calculations on the input data, followed by a thread which controls a valve. Then the sensor thread runs again.

2.9.1 Priority

In an interactive system there is no way to predict in advance how many threads will be running, or how long they will want to run for. They could be scheduled on a first come, first served basis. But this way some unimportant threads could monopolize the system, while urgent threads languish on a queue.

So a common practice is to order all of the runnable or ready threads by some priority criterion. There could be any number of priorities, typically 8, 16 or 32. The simplest way to think about it is that this priority is allocated to the thread when it is created. The descriptors of all runnable threads are linked into the run queue, ordered by decreasing priority. The most eligible thread is at the head, then the next, and so on. All the other threads, which are not runnable, are linked together on the wait queue. The situation is illustrated in Figure 2.14. But remember that the `thread` structures shown here do not exist in isolation – each one is part of the process descriptor of the process it belongs to.

Figure 2.14 Threads on the ready and wait queues

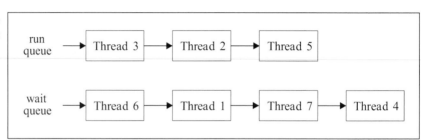

> Modern CPUs tend to have a special privileged register which points to the data structure representing the current running thread.

Each thread gets a certain time slice on the processor. This is called the quantum. Each time the hardware timer interrupts, the scheduler decrements the quantum. When it gets to zero, it is time to context switch. If a thread is still runnable when its time is up, the context switcher moves it to the appropriate position in the queue, depending on its priority.

> Most systems now use separate queues for each priority. The thread at the head of the highest priority non-empty queue will always be the next to run. When a thread is preempted, it is moved to the tail of its queue. This is known as round robin scheduling.

2.9.2 Multilevel priority queues

A system must allow for the possibility of the priority changing over time. For example, consider a system with only two priorities, high and low, as illustrated in Figure 2.15. Interactive threads would be given high priority – they need to be able to respond quickly to external events, such as a key being pressed. Compute-bound threads, such as compilations, can be given low priority. Nobody is going to get upset if it takes a second or two longer.

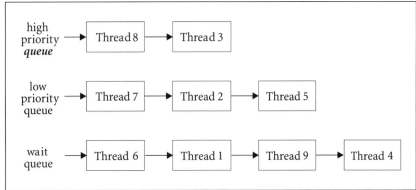

Figure 2.15 Two different priority queues

When a thread is created, it is initially put on the high-priority queue. If it uses its full time slice this implies that it is compute-bound. So when it is context switched out, it is moved to the tail of the low-priority queue. On the other hand, if the thread gives up the processor to wait for an I/O event, then it can be assumed that it is interactive. Then when the event it is waiting for occurs, it is moved from the wait queue to the high-priority queue. Threads on this queue are always offered the processor before the low-priority queue, but are expected to keep it for a shorter time.

The situation described can be generalized to any number of priorities, with a thread migrating between them. Typically, different queues would have different time slices. I/O bound threads would have high priority, and hence receive rapid service. But they would have short time slices, because it is unlikely that they will do much processing before giving up the processor and waiting for more I/O.

On the other hand, CPU-bound threads have lower priorities; hence they have to wait longer between turns on the CPU. But they would have longer time slices, so when they do get the processor they can make significant use of it.

The information needed to manage this is kept in the `thread` structure. The base priority and maximum priority are decided when it is created. This would probably depend on the importance of the owner of the process. The final field in the `thread` structure of Figure 2.8 always contains the current priority of the thread.

CHAPTER SUMMARY

▶ A process is the unit of work in a computer system. It consists of a task, or set of system resources, such as a program and memory space, and a thread, or control path through the program.

▶ As there is normally only one processor, it is shared among all processes.

▶ It is becoming common to allow more than one control path, or thread, through the one program. This reduces the non-productive overhead involved in frequently saving and restoring the state of the machine.

▶ The system keeps track of each process by means of a data structure called a process descriptor. In practice this can be a collection of structures, each representing one aspect of the process.

▶ In POSIX, new processes are created as almost exact clones of their parents. The main differences are that they have an identification number of their own, and have only one thread. When a process terminates, it can send status information back to its parent.

▶ Further threads can then be created to run within that process.

▶ At any given time, a thread will either be runnable or waiting.

▶ When a processor is being reallocated from one thread to another, it is necessary to save the current state of the machine and restore the previously saved state.

▶ The decision as to which thread to run next is known as scheduling. This could be on a first come, first served, run to completion basis. More commonly, a variation of this is used, where each thread gets a maximum amount of time, the quantum. If it does not finish within the quantum, it is context switched out and put at the back of the queue.

Even more typically, priority schemes are used, with a different queue of ready threads for each priority. The priority of a thread can be dynamically adjusted to reflect its historical use of the CPU.

FURTHER READING

General background on process management can be found in Silberschatz and Galvin Section 4.1; Nutt Chapter 6; Tanenbaum and Woodhull Section 2.1; Stallings Chapter 3; Tanenbaum (1992) Section 2.1. For more on process creation see Silberschatz and Galvin Section 4.3. Rago Chapter 2 is a very good introduction to POSIX system programming; Robbins and Robbins Appendix A, and Gray Chapter 1 also cover the same material, and Gray introduces manual pages in Appendix A. The fork() system call is described in Robbins and Robbins Chapter 2; Grey Chapter 3; Stevens Chapter 8. For more information on threads see Silberschatz and Galvin Section 4.5; Tanenbaum (1992) Section 12.1. For threads programming see Robbins and Robbins Chapter 9. Scheduling is dealt with in Silberschatz and Galvin Section 4.2 and Chapter 5; Nutt Chapter 7; Tanenbaum and Woodhull Section 2.4; Stallings Chapter 8; Tanenbaum (1992) Section 2.4.

SELF-TEST QUESTIONS

1 Distinguish between the static part of a process (the task) and the dynamic part (the thread).

2 How can more than one thread be executing at the same time on a machine with only one CPU?

3   What is the motivation behind introducing multiple threads of control in the one process?

4   Outline the fields in the data structures used to represent a process, a task and a thread within an operating system.

5   Explain how the POSIX `fork()` function creates a new process.

6   Explain the difference between calling a function and creating a new thread to execute that function.

7   Outline the life cycle of a thread.

8   Explain how context switching works.

9   Describe the different objectives of a scheduler in interactive, batch and real-time systems.

10   Explain what is meant by priority scheduling.

11   Explain how multilevel priority feedback queues work.

DISCUSSION QUESTIONS

1   Figure 2.3 is an oversimplification. Redraw it to include a row representing the operating system itself.

2   When a process moves from running to idle, the state of the machine has to be saved. Obviously this cannot mean the whole state, as there would be no place to save it. Does the task have to be saved? Would it be sufficient just to save information about the thread?

3   One way of implementing a multi-threaded server would be to have a boss thread, which gives out jobs to a number of worker threads. Discuss the trade-offs involved in having a fixed number of these, as opposed to creating a new one for each job and terminating it when finished.

4   Process descriptors could be kept on hash queues. How would this compare for efficiency with static tables and linked lists?

5   The information about open files is kept in the `task` structure. What would be the effect of putting this in the `thread` structure instead?

6   Some operating systems create a new process as a clone of the existing one; others create a new process with a new program. Discuss the advantages and disadvantages of both systems.

7   What would happen if the `fork()` system call were inside a loop?

8   Investigate the `wait()` and `exit()` system services. What happens if a child calls `exit()`, but the parent never calls `wait()`?

9   Investigate the `getpid()` and `getppid()` system services. Why do you think there is no system service which returns the id of a child process?

10   Investigate the different versions of the `exec()` system service, and distinguish between them.

11   The perror() library function should never be used with thread functions. Why not?

12   What is the difference between a function recursively calling itself and a function creating a new thread to run another copy of itself?

13   Investigate how to pass parameters to a thread when creating it.

14   List all the possible combinations of terminating and detaching which result in the thread structure being removed.

15   What would happen to a process if all of its threads terminate and are detached?

16   When the context switcher is running, the PC holds an address within context switcher code, so it would not be correct to save the actual contents of the PC. What is really required is to save the contents of the PC as it was just before the context switcher ran. How can this be done?

17   Modern CPUs have special instructions to do all of the copying of registers required at a context switch. Investigate these instructions for a machine of your choice.

18   What happens if a thread uses up its quantum but is still the highest priority thread in the whole system? How is this situation avoided with multilevel feedback queues?

Concurrency

The aim of this chapter is to consider the implications of having more than one thread executing at the same time, and to examine some of the solutions which have been developed to control interaction between threads.

After reading this chapter, you should:

- ▶ be familiar with the implications of cooperation and competition between concurrent threads
- ▶ understand the semaphore mechanism and its associated operations WAIT and SIGNAL
- ▶ be able to apply semaphores in the standard situations: mutual exclusion, synchronization, resource management, bounded buffer
- ▶ understand how semaphores might be implemented within an operating system
- ▶ be familiar with the message-passing mechanism
- ▶ be familiar with monitors
- ▶ understand the deadlock implications of concurrent threads

3.1 Introduction

The previous chapter introduced the concept of a process as the unit of work within a computer system. It has also introduced the concept of one or more threads of control in each process. We have seen that it is possible, even likely, that many threads will be in existence at the same time, belonging to different processes. Each will be somewhere between its initial state and its final state. Such threads are said to be concurrent, running at the same time. As there is typically only one processor, we only have apparent concurrency, with the operating system switching between whichever thread has control at any one time.

If the threads are unrelated, and never need to interact in any way, then there should be no problem. But frequently they do need to work together to achieve the goal of the concurrent system. For example, many threads may each generate part of a solution; these parts then need to be combined.

So, the operating system must be able to provide for, and control, interaction between concurrent threads.

3.2 Interaction between threads

Let us begin by looking at why threads may need to interact with each other.

3.2.1 Cooperation

Threads may need to cooperate to carry out some particular job. For example, one thread may make a request for service on some other thread. It then has to wait for the service to be done. A user thread may request an operating system thread to read from a disk drive. It has to wait for the data to be available in memory before proceeding.

In cases like this, there is a general requirement for some mechanism by which a thread can wait to synchronize with another thread, or with the hardware. The other side of this is that one thread must be able to signal to another thread that some point is reached, or that some particular piece of work has been carried out.

3.2.2 Competition

Concurrent threads may compete for exclusive use of resources. They may make simultaneous requests for the same resource or the same service.

As an example to illustrate the basic problem, consider a producer thread which puts items onto a linked list and a consumer thread which takes them off. Several pointers have to be changed when inserting or removing an item on a linked list. They cannot all be changed simultaneously, so there is always a short time when the links are inconsistent.

Now suppose that the producer is context-switched out at just that inconsistent point, and the consumer context switched in. At best, an item will be lost or an item will be read twice. At worst, the consumer may hang, or it may even crash the operating system.

The problem can be summarized as follows. We have a number of concurrent threads. Each has a segment of code, called its *critical section*, in which it is executing instructions which may affect other threads, e.g. updating common variables. We must be able to ensure that when one thread is executing in its critical section no other thread can be executing in its critical section. Another way of putting this is that execution of critical sections must be mutually exclusive in time.

3.2.3 Software solutions

Historically, the problem of mutual exclusion was first tackled in software. Attempts were made to design a protocol, or a set of rules and regulations, that programmers would write into the code being executed by each thread and which would guarantee that only one thread was in its critical section at any one time.

In general, a program would have the format shown in Figure 3.1. Of course, this whole structure may be within a loop. But a program will never branch into or out of the critical section.

Figure 3.1 General structure of a
cooperating program

beginning section

Entry protocol for critical section
critical section
Exit protocol for critical section

remainder section

These software solutions are rarely, if ever, used nowadays. But a study of these algorithms is well worth the effort involved, as it leads to a thorough understanding of the pitfalls involved in concurrent programming. We will not consider this any further, but the algorithms can be found in any of the major texts on operating systems.

There are significant difficulties with all of these algorithms.

▶ They all rely on continuous testing of variables, or busy waiting, which is very wasteful of CPU cycles.

▶ All of the details have to be implemented by each individual programmer, and the possibility of programmer error is always there.

▶ More seriously, there is no way to enforce the protocol. It depends on cooperation. A programmer may omit part of it, or leave it out altogether and just go directly to the critical section.

▶ Apart from all of that, these protocols are just too complicated.

So programmers began to demand that the operating system help with concurrency problems. One of the reasons why operating systems exist at all is to provide a more user-friendly environment for a programmer.

In the following sections we will examine several mechanisms which operating system designers have provided to help with these problems.

3.3 Semaphores

The first such general solution was a mechanism called a semaphore. This can be described as:

a non-negative integer, which apart from initialisation, can be acted on only by two standard, atomic, un-interruptible operations, WAIT (which decrements the value of the semaphore) and SIGNAL (which increments the value).

Instead of users trying to devise their own synchronization protocols, semaphores are provided as a tool by the system implementor.

Using semaphores, competing or collaborating threads do not have to know even the number of contenders, much less their identities or internal implementation details. All they have to know is the *name* of the semaphore.

3.3.1 WAIT

A WAIT operation decreases the value of the semaphore by 1 in one indivisible operation. But it can only do that if the result would be non-negative. If the value of the semaphore before the WAIT is 0, then the thread cannot continue and is moved to a wait queue.

A WAIT is not the same as assignment, s = s − 1. If two threads WAIT on a semaphore with a value of 3, it is guaranteed that the value afterwards will be 1. If two threads use assignment statements to decrement a shared variable with a value of 3, the final result may be 1 or 2. This is because the assignment statement will typically compile to three machine instructions: a copy to a register, decrement the register, and a copy back to memory.

```
ld items, r0
dec r0
st r0, items
```

One thread could be swapped out after the first instruction, or the second, and another thread could complete an assignment, setting the value of the variable to 2. When the first thread runs again and completes the assignment, it too will set the variable to 2.

Note that it is not possible to read the value of the semaphore (although some implementations have provided for this).

3.3.2 SIGNAL

A SIGNAL operation increases the value of the semaphore by 1, again in an indivisible operation.

However, if there is even one thread waiting on the semaphore, SIGNAL has a different effect. It wakes up that thread, marks it runnable and moves it to a run queue.

3.4 Applications of semaphores

Having introduced the idea of a semaphore, we now go on to see how they can be used to solve various concurrency problems. We will then look at how they are implemented.

3.4.1 Semaphores for mutual exclusion

To arrange for mutual exclusion, a single semaphore, initialized to 1, is used. Here the semaphore is called *Guard*. A commonly used name for a mutual exclusion semaphore is *Mutex*.

Each thread uses it as shown in Figure 3.2. Note that the entry protocol is simply a WAIT, while the exit protocol is a SIGNAL.

Figure 3.2 Semaphore for mutual exclusion

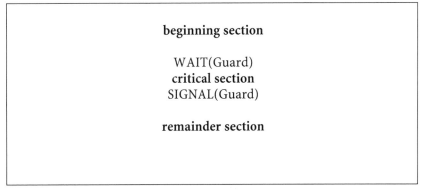

beginning section

WAIT(Guard)
critical section
SIGNAL(Guard)

remainder section

The state of the semaphore immediately after initialisation is shown in Figure 3.3(a). The value is 1, and there are no threads on the wait queue.

Figure 3.3 Successive states of a mutual exclusion semaphore

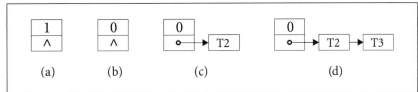

After the first contending thread has done a WAIT, the value of the semaphore is 0. The state of the semaphore is now as in Figure 3.3(b).

If a second thread then does a WAIT, the semaphore is not decremented further, but that thread is blocked and put on the semaphore wait queue, as in Figure 3.3(c). Any subsequent threads that WAIT on that semaphore are added to the tail of that queue (Figure 3.3(d)).

When the first thread leaves its critical section and does a SIGNAL on the semaphore, one of the waiting threads is woken up, and moved from the wait queue to the run queue. The value of the semaphore is unchanged.

When that thread does a SIGNAL in turn, another is woken up, and so on. Eventually there will be no threads on the queue and the semaphore will have a value of 0, as in Figure 3.3(b). Then the final thread does a SIGNAL and the value is restored to 1, as in Figure 3.3(a).

Note that the correct working of the mutual exclusion algorithm depends on all of the programmers doing everything correctly. If anyone omits a WAIT or a SIGNAL, or inserts an extra WAIT or SIGNAL, then mutual exclusion will not be guaranteed.

3.4.2   Semaphores for synchronisation

The requirement here is that thread A must not pass a point P1 in its code until thread B has reached a point P2 in its code. For example, A may require an item at P1 which is only provided by B at P2.

The solution is to use one semaphore, S, initialized to 0.

There are two possible scenarios. The first is shown in Figure 3.4(a). Thread A may get to P1 before B gets to P2. In that case, when A executes

Figure 3.4 Semaphore for synchronisation

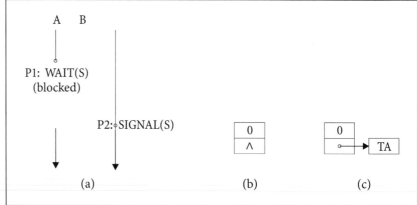

a WAIT on the semaphore it is blocked (on a 0 valued semaphore) and put on a wait queue. The semaphore changes from the state shown in Figure 3.4(b) to 3.4(c). When B eventually gets to P2, and does a SIGNAL on the semaphore, A will be woken up and continue execution. The semaphore returns to the state in Figure 3.4(b). Note that the value of the semaphore is always 0 in this case.

The other possibility is that B can get to P2 before A gets to P1. This is shown in Figure 3.5(a). In this case, the value of the semaphore is incremented to 1. It changes from the state shown in Figure 3.5(b) to 3.5(c). Then when A does a WAIT, it is not held up, but the semaphore is decremented to 0, and returns to the state shown in Figure 3.5(b).

Figure 3.5 An alternative for synchronisation

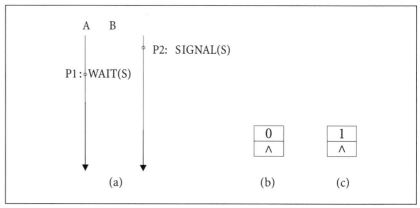

If the two threads were running on a multiprocessor, then they could attempt to WAIT and SIGNAL at exactly the same time. It is left to the implementation to decide which goes first. Remember that the definition of a semaphore requires that WAIT and SIGNAL be indivisible. So there is no possibility of their being interleaved.

3.4.3 Semaphores for resource management

Semaphores can be used to control the allocation and deallocation of resources. These can be physical resources, such as printers, but they can also be virtual resources such as slots in a buffer.

The semaphore is initialized to the number of instances available. A thread requests a resource by a WAIT on the semaphore. As long as there is a resource available it will not be held up. Eventually, when all resources have been allocated, the value of the semaphore will be 0. Any further threads requesting a resource by doing a WAIT on that semaphore will be blocked and put on a wait queue.

A thread returns a resource by a SIGNAL on the semaphore. If no thread is waiting, then the value of the semaphore (number of instances available) will be incremented. If there are threads waiting, then one will be woken up and given the newly returned resource.

3.5 Producers and consumers

There is a whole class of problems in which producer threads place data in a buffer and consumer threads take it out. This has both synchronization and mutual exclusion implications. A thread attempting to take data from an empty buffer must block. A thread putting data into a full buffer must also block. And always the buffer must be protected from simultaneous access by more than one thread.

In the following examples, we will assume a circular buffer with N fixed-size slots, numbered 1 to N. After slot N has been filled (or emptied), the next slot to be used is slot 1 again.

Figure 3.6 shows an eight slot buffer, on the left as it would actually be laid out in memory, and on the right as it might be envisaged in the algorithms which follow.

Figure 3.6 Circular buffer with eight slots

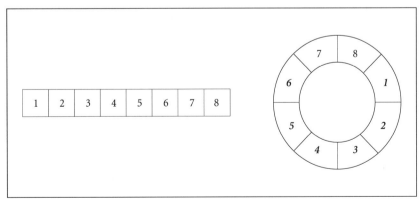

3.5.1 One producer, one consumer

We will begin with a situation in which there is only one producer thread, and likewise one consumer thread.

This needs two semaphores, SlotFree, which is initialized to the maximum number of slots in the buffer, and ItemAvailable, which is initialized to 0, as there are 0 items available at initialisation time. These values reflect the initial state of the system. At any given time, the value of ItemAvailable is the number of unconsumed items in the buffer and the value of SlotFree is the number of free slots available for use.

There are also two pointers. NextIn points to the next slot in the buffer to be used by the producer. NextOut points to the slot from which the consumer is to take the next item. Both are initialized to point to the first slot. When each of these gets to the end of the buffer, it wraps around to point to the first slot again. This complication is omitted from the algorithms, which stress rather the use of semaphores.

Producer

The algorithm for the producer is given in Figure 3.7.

Figure 3.7 Algorithm for producer

```
Produce an Item
WAIT(SlotFree)
Put Item in Buffer at NextIn
Increment NextIn
SIGNAL(ItemAvailable)
```

Consumer

The corresponding algorithm for the consumer is given in Figure 3.8.

Figure 3.8 Algorithm for consumer

```
WAIT(ItemAvailable)
Get Item from Buffer at NextOut
Increment NextOut
SIGNAL(SlotFree)
Consume the Item
```

When the buffer is empty, the consumer will be held up by the WAIT on ItemAvailable, which is 0. It will only get past this point when the producer does a SIGNAL on ItemAvailable, which it only does after depositing an item in the buffer.

When the buffer is full, the producer will be held up by the WAIT on SlotFree, which now has a value of 0. It will only get past this point when the consumer does a SIGNAL on SlotFree, which it will only do after it has removed an item from the buffer, thus making a slot available for reuse.

Mutual exclusion

There is no mutual exclusion semaphore in the implementation given here. This may seem to contradict previous statements that, to avoid interference, threads should only access shared resources under mutual exclusion. But in this case, the structure of the code, and the fact that there are only two threads, guarantees that they cannot be accessing the same slot at the same time. It is worthwhile considering this in some detail, as it helps to understand some of the implications of using a shared buffer.

Both threads can only be accessing the same slot in the buffer at the same time when NextIn and NextOut have the same value, and are therefore pointing to the same slot.

There are only two possible ways in which this can happen. One is when the buffer is empty and NextIn and NextOut are both pointing at the next empty slot: the producer to put in there as soon as something is produced, and the consumer to take from there as soon as something is put in. In this case the consumer is held up by the semaphore ItemAvailable, and so cannot get on to the line where it takes from the buffer. Before the producer does a SIGNAL on this semaphore, it will already have finished with this slot, and moved NextIn to point to the next slot.

The other possibility is when the buffer is full, and both are looking at the next full slot: the producer to put in there as soon as it becomes available, the consumer to take from there as soon as it is ready for another item. In this case the producer is held up on the semaphore SlotFree, and cannot get on to the line where it actually uses the buffer. Before the consumer does a SIGNAL on this semaphore, it will already have finished with this slot and incremented NextOut to point to the following slot.

While a mutual exclusion semaphore is not strictly required in this example, it is probably good practice always to include one when there is a shared resource involved.

3.5.2 Multiple producers, multiple consumers

We use the same two semaphores, and pointers, as in the previous example. But in this case we must introduce a mutual exclusion semaphore, *Guard*, initialized to 1. This is because two or more producers could try to put an item into the same slot at the same time, or two consumers could try to take from the same slot at the same time.

The algorithm for a producer is given in Figure 3.9, and that for a consumer in Figure 3.10. All of the comments on the previous pair of algorithms apply here.

Figure 3.9 Algorithm for one of many producers

```
Produce an item
WAIT(SlotFree)
WAIT(Guard)
Put item in buffer at NextIn
Increment NextIn
SIGNAL(Guard)
SIGNAL(ItemAvailable)
```

Figure 3.10 Algorithm for one of
many consumers

WAIT(ItemAvailable)
WAIT(Guard)
Get item from buffer at NextOut
Increment NextOut
SIGNAL(Guard)
SIGNAL(SlotFree)
Consume the item

With only one Guard, only one thread, producer or consumer, can be active in the buffer at any time. It would be possible to have two mutual exclusion semaphores. One would be for producers, to guarantee that only one producer could be putting an item into the buffer at any one time. The second semaphore would be for consumers, and would guarantee that only one consumer could be getting an item from the buffer at any one time. In this case, one producer and one consumer could be active in the buffer at the same time. They would be prevented from operating on the same slot by the reasoning of the previous subsection.

Note that the order in which a WAIT is done on the semaphores in both algorithms is critical. If a producer did the WAIT on Guard before the WAIT on SlotFree, and the buffer were full, no consumer could get past the WAIT on Guard and the system would deadlock.

Likewise, if a consumer did a WAIT on Guard before the WAIT on ItemAvailable, and the buffer were empty, no producer could get past the WAIT on Guard and the system would deadlock.

3.6 Implementation of semaphores

There are many elements involved in the actual implementation of a semaphore.

Apart from the incrementing or decrementing of the semaphore value, there is the interaction with the scheduler implied by the requirement that a thread doing a WAIT on a zero-valued semaphore must not continue processing. Then there is a question of how to keep track of all of the threads waiting on a particular semaphore. A SIGNAL on a semaphore with threads waiting on it also has implications for the scheduler. Finally, probably the most significant aspect of the implementation is the requirement that all of this be done as one single uninterruptible operation.

We will first of all look at indivisibility and then at the implementation of semaphore operations.

3.6.1 Indivisibility of operation

The critical aspect of operations on semaphores is that they are executed atomically. The implementation must guarantee that no two threads can operate on the same semaphore at the same time. So the code for both WAIT and SIGNAL must begin with some form of LOCK and finish with an UNLOCK.

On a uniprocessor, this could be implemented by disabling interrupts and enabling them again when finished. In this way a thread cannot lose control of the CPU. Hence WAIT and SIGNAL are indivisible. But the implementation of WAIT or SIGNAL might run to 20 or 30 machine instructions. It is not really acceptable to have the machine running with interrupts disabled for such a long time.

So some other solution has to be found. Just as previously the application programmers threw the problem back at the operating system designers, so now these latter throw the problem back at the hardware designers. We ask them to include some mechanism in the hardware specifically for this purpose.

Different hardware designers have come up with different ways to implement such a lock.

One possibility is a machine-level instruction which, in one operation, exchanges the contents of two locations. With this, LOCK is implemented as shown in Figure 3.11. Key is a global variable; each thread would have its own copy of Local. If the value in Key is 1, this means that another thread is holding the lock and the current one cannot proceed. If the value of Key is 0, then the semaphore is free and the current thread can proceed. If there is a value of 1 in Local after the Exchange, this means that the Key was 1 beforehand. Only when there is a value of 0 in Local after the Exchange can you be sure that Key was 0 beforehand.

Figure 3.11 Lock using exchange

```
REPEAT
   Local = 1
   Exchange(Local, Key)
UNTIL Local == 0
```

The UNLOCK routine is a simple assignment, Key = 0. Any compiler will produce one uninterruptible machine-level instruction for this.

> Intel microprocessors have an XCHG instruction which exchanges the contents of a register with a memory location. So Key would be in memory, while Local would be in a register.

This LOCK mechanism goes around the REPEAT loop continually until it finds a value of 0 in Key. This is known as busy waiting. But as long as the implementation of WAIT and SIGNAL are simple, the time spent busy waiting should be reasonably short. Any contending threads should execute the code for WAIT and SIGNAL and release the lock in a very short space of time, so there should be virtually no busy waiting.

On the other hand, application programs may have very long critical sections, which are almost always occupied. Figure 3.12 tries to illustrate the timing relationship of LOCK and UNLOCK to WAIT and SIGNAL.

It is not possible to use LOCK and UNLOCK in place of WAIT and SIGNAL. Busy waiting is not acceptable over the time-scale involved.

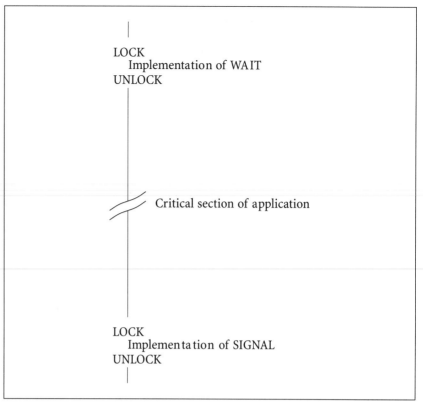

Figure 3.12 Timing relationship of locks and semaphores

3.6.2   Implementation of WAIT

Decrementing the semaphore value is trivial. When a thread does a WAIT on a zero-valued semaphore it must be blocked and moved from the run queue to a semaphore queue. This means that, as well as a value, the semaphore data structure must also contain a pointer to the head of a queue. The queue itself is implemented by a link field in each `thread` descriptor. This could possibly be the same field as used for the run queue, as a thread can never be waiting on a semaphore and runnable at the same time.

Our implementation is shown in Figure 3.13.

Figure 3.13 Implementation of WAIT

```
LOCK (Key)
IF s == 0 THEN
   Mark current thread sleeping
   Move from run queue to semaphore queue
   UNLOCK(Key)
   Call scheduler
ELSE
   Decrement s
   UNLOCK(Key)
ENDIF
```

It is absolutely necessary that the UNLOCK comes before the call to the scheduler. Otherwise a context switch could take place without the LOCK being released. Some other thread trying to perform a semaphore operation could then be held up (unnecessarily) when it tries to LOCK(Key).

3.6.3 Implementation of signal

The implementation of SIGNAL is given in Figure 3.14.

Figure 3.14 Implementation of SIGNAL

```
LOCK(Key)
   IF there is a thread on the queue THEN
   Mark first waiting thread runnable
   Move from semaphore queue to run queue
ELSE
   Increment s
ENDIF
UNLOCK (Key)
```

The only complication arises if there are some threads waiting on the semaphore. If so, then action must be taken to wake up a sleeping thread.

POSIX semaphores

POSIX introduced a standard operating system interface to semaphores. While there is only one semaphore mechanism implemented, there are two interfaces supplied to this. The two varieties are described as unnamed semaphores and named semaphores. The basic distinction between them is that while unnamed semaphores can only be used within one process or between related processes, named semaphores can also be used by totally unrelated processes. All they need to know is the name of the semaphore.

An unnamed semaphore is created and initialized by a call to sem_init(). A parameter specifies the initial value of the semaphore. Once created, it can be used by any thread in the process.

A named semaphore is identified system-wide by its name. The system service sem_open() can be used either to create a new semaphore, or to associate an already existing semaphore with the calling process.

3.7 Limitations of semaphores

It may seem that all concurrency problems have been solved at this stage. But semaphores are not perfect. The following are some of the areas in which the semaphore mechanism (at least as described here) is deficient.

1   Their use is not enforced – it is by convention only. Programmers can accidentally or deliberately not use them, and violate mutual exclusion.

2   Incorrect use can cause deadlock, as noted when dealing with multiple producers and consumers.

3 A low-priority thread can acquire a mutual exclusion semaphore and hold it locked against all others, no matter how high their priority. Because it is of low priority, it is also likely to be preempted while holding the semaphore. This phenomenon is known as 'priority inversion', when the lowest priority thread is holding up all of the others.

4 The semaphore mechanism does not actually pass any data. This has to be arranged separately, e.g. using a shared buffer.

5 Blocking is indefinite; it is not possible to specify a timeout.

6 It is not possible to specify waiting on two or more semaphores with AND/OR conditions.

The semaphore mechanism can be improved (at the cost of extra complexity), particularly to cater for points 5 and 6. But in general, we have to continue our search for other mechanisms.

3.8 Message passing

Semaphores only dealt with the mutual exclusion and synchronization aspects of interprocess communication. Any data transferred between threads had to be catered for separately from this, typically by using buffers in shared memory.

One possible development to take from these low-level primitives is to make them more powerful by combining data transfer with mutual exclusion and synchronization. This can be implemented by some form of structured message passing. The system would arrange for both the transfer of such messages between threads (as well as synchronization between sender and receiver) and the queueing of messages where required.

Some argue that message passing should always be used, as it is a mechanism which extends neatly to distributed systems.

Such a message-passing system can be asynchronous or synchronous.

3.8.1 Asynchronous message passing

With this type of message passing, a sending thread is never delayed. Sending a message need not be immediately followed by receiving – the operating system can maintain a queue of waiting messages.

Figure 3.15 gives the outline of a message passing system. Note that the operating system is involved in all data passing between the two threads. They never communicate directly with each other, only with the operating system. But both threads take the initiative; the operating system does not force messages on the receiver.

3.8.2 Synchronous message passing

Message passing can also be implemented in such a way that the sender and receiver must first synchronize, and then the message is copied from one to the other. This avoids the overhead of any buffer management.

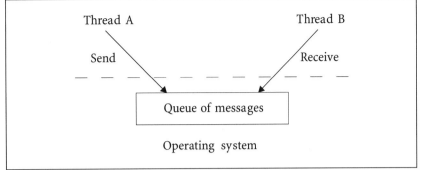

Figure 3.15 Outline of message passing

However, this type of message passing is not always suitable. Because the receiver must always be ready and waiting, an important server process could be blocked while trying to send a reply, when it could and should be going ahead with work for others.

In a multi-threaded environment, one possible solution would be for the client to create a new thread to handle each request. This sends the request to the server and then blocks, waiting for the reply. Other client threads can continue execution. The blocked thread is always ready and waiting when the server wants to reply.

3.8.3 POSIX message queues

A POSIX message queue is basically a linked list of messages. The boundaries between messages are clearly distinguished by the system; you do not have to know the length of a message in advance. Messages can also be given priorities and read out of sequence, and the sender and receiver do not have to share a common ancestor.

They have their own set of system services. A process creates a message queue, or connects to an existing one, with `mq_open()`. The particular queue is specified by name.

The `mq_send()` system service is used to send a message. It is possible to specify a priority for the message being sent. A thread attempting to send a message on a full queue will block.

The `mq_receive()` system service returns the oldest, highest priority message and its priority. A thread trying to read from an empty queue will block.

> But there are still some features which could be added to POSIX message queues. It is not possible to specify a receiver when sending a message. Any thread with access to the message queue can read any message. Nor is there any broadcast mechanism. The first thread to read a message removes it from the queue, and it is no longer available to any others.

It is not really feasible to have duplex communication with a message queue. If one thread did a send, followed immediately by a receive, then it would get its own message back. Such duplex communication is normally implemented by using two queues, one for each direction.

3.9 Monitors

The low-level primitives discussed so far, semaphores and message queues, do not guarantee that they will be used correctly. Undisciplined use of any of these mechanisms can lead to errors, as we have seen. Even when legitimately allowed to access a resource, a thread may corrupt it erroneously or maliciously. The message-passing mechanism cannot detect invalid or illegal messages.

An even better solution would be a programming language construct which forces a programmer to declare explicitly what data is shared and where the critical sections are in a program. With this information, a compiler could check and enforce that shared data is only accessed from within a critical section, and that critical sections are mutually exclusive.

Monitors were developed to provide this facility. The basic idea of a monitor is to provide data abstraction or data hiding. It consists of the shared data and one or more functions. The critical data is accessible indirectly and exclusively through this set of functions. This controls the nature of operations performed on the data to prevent meaningless or potentially harmful updates.

The critical region and data declarations in each application program are replaced by a call to a monitor procedure. Users have no way of knowing the internal organisation of a monitor, such as the number, identity or structure of variables or functions.

3.9.1 Mutual exclusion

In order to guarantee that there is mutual exclusion on the data, the implementation of a monitor must also ensure that only one thread is active in the monitor at any time. This is implemented by a mutual exclusion semaphore inserted by the compiler. Because of this, calling a monitor procedure may imply a delay.

3.9.2 Synchronization

Apart from mutual exclusion, synchronization is also needed within the monitor. For example, if a monitor controls a shared buffer, at times this buffer may be full, and a producer thread should not be allowed to continue. Such synchronization could also be arranged using semaphores. But we have seen problems with this, where a thread waiting on a synchronisation semaphore, and holding a mutual exclusion semaphore, could prevent other threads from synchronising with it, and so lead to deadlock.

Condition variables

Because of this, a variant of a semaphore, known as a condition variable, has been developed especially for use within monitors. Condition variables allow a thread, under the protection of guaranteed exclusive access, to test some arbitrary programmer-specified condition, and decide whether to block itself or not. It blocks and gives up the mutual exclusion in one atomic action.

Whenever a thread changes the state of one of the shared variables, it signals the condition variable. The signal means only that the value of the variable has changed, not that the condition is true. This wakes up a waiting thread and gives it mutual exclusion on the monitor. This thread can then check to see if the condition it is waiting on is now TRUE. If not, it waits again on that condition variable, releasing the mutual exclusion.

Unlike a semaphore, a condition variable is implemented as a header to a queue of waiting processes. There is no integer. There are only two operations on such condition variables, CWAIT and CSIGNAL.

Waiting on a condition variable

Figure 3.16 illustrates what happens when a thread calls CWAIT – it always blocks itself and calls the scheduler to give the CPU to some other thread. This is different from WAIT on a semaphore, which only blocks when the value is 0. It remains blocked until some other thread does a CSIGNAL. But note that it also releases mutual exclusion on the monitor while it is blocked.

Figure 3.16 Implementation of CWAIT

```
LOCK
    Mark thread un-runnable
    Queue the thread on the condition variable
    Release mutual exclusion on the monitor
UNLOCK
Call scheduler
```

Signalling a condition variable

Figure 3.17 illustrates what happens when a process calls CSIGNAL. It has an effect only if there is at least one thread waiting. This is different from a SIGNAL on a semaphore, which always has some effect, either waking a thread up or incrementing the value.

Figure 3.17 Implementation of CSIGNAL

```
LOCK
IF there is a thread waiting on condition variable
THEN
    Mark one runnable
    Mark current thread un-runnable
    Transfer mutual exclusion on the monitor to
    selected thread
ENDIF
UNLOCK
Return
```

As CSIGNAL causes the thread executing it to give up the mutual exclusion on the monitor, normally it is the last instruction executed by a function before leaving the monitor. The compiler enforces this.

> Condition variables are part of the POSIX `pthread` package.

Figure 3.18 illustrates the different parts of a Monitor.

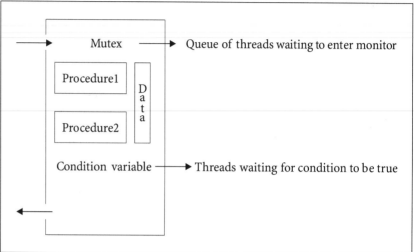

Figure 3.18 An illustration of a monitor

> The programming of monitor procedures still needs great care. But it is only done once, hopefully by a specialist and competent programmer. Ordinary programmers only have to call procedures and pass parameters. They have no need to worry about mutual exclusion or synchronization.

3.9.3 Example using a monitor

We will now look at how an allocator for a single resource could be implemented using a monitor (see Figure 3.19). This simple monitor could be used to control allocation of a printer, for example. We have already seen this implemented with a semaphore. Note that there is no express mention of mutual exclusion. This is all taken care of by the compiler once it sees the keyword MONITOR.

The use of a `while` in `reserve()` means that when the thread is woken up after the CWAIT it will test the condition one more time before going on and claiming the resource.

Remember that no part of the implementation shown here would be visible to a user. All the user would know would be the names of the two functions, `reserve()` and `release()`, and the effect of calling them. When control returns from a call to `reserve()`, the thread has

Figure 3.19 Monitor to allocate a single resource

```
MONITOR allocator
{
boolean busy = false;
condition free;

reserve()
  {
  while (busy == true)
    CWAIT(free);
  busy = true;
  }

release()
  {
  busy = false;
  CSIGNAL(free);
  }
}
```

exclusive rights to the resource. When control returns from a call to `release()`, the thread no longer has any rights to the resource.

> Note that the actual resource is not in the monitor; there is nothing in this implementation to prevent an unscrupulous programmer from accessing the resource without permission.

Other problems, such as the bounded buffer manager and readers/writers, can also be solved using monitors. Examples can be found in the standard operating systems textbooks.

3.9.4   Disadvantages of monitors

The advantages of monitors have been outlined already, but there is also a downside.

1   The fact that only one thread can be active in the monitor at any one time can be restrictive. One solution is for the shared resources to be outside the monitor, which controls only the granting and taking back of permissions to access the resource, as in Figure 3.19. But this does not *enforce* mutual exclusion.

2   As with semaphores, a thread calling a monitor is committed to wait if the monitor is in use, and again if the resource is not available.
    One possible solution to this is to create a child thread which calls the monitor, while the parent thread proceeds in parallel. Of course at some stage the parent has to be assured that the work has been done, so there is a need for synchronization between them.

3.10 Deadlock

Before leaving the subject of concurrency, we must give some consideration to the problem of deadlock between threads in concurrent processes. While resources are always requested by some particular thread, they are held by the process and are available to all threads in that process. So it would be very unusual for threads in the same process to deadlock among themselves. This normally occurs between threads in *different* processes.

The simplest possible example of deadlock would involve two threads and two files. Each thread has one of the files open for exclusive writing, and each wants to open the other. They will both wait forever.

A more formal definition would be:

> A set of threads is in a deadlock state when every thread in the set is waiting on a resource which is being held by another thread in the set.

Note first of all that every thread is waiting; if even one of them was runnable, then the set would not be deadlocked. Note also that all of the resources being waited on are held by a thread or threads within the set. If even one of the resources was held by some thread outside the set, then they would not be deadlocked.

3.10.1 Resource types and instances

Resources are divided into different *types*. There can be any number of identical *instances* of a particular type. If a thread requests an instance of a resource type, the request can be satisfied by allocating any instance of that type.

Normally, the following sequence must be followed: request, which may result in a wait; followed eventually by allocation; followed by use; followed by release. It is taken for granted that a thread may not use a resource without first requesting and being granted it, and that a thread will always return a resource after use.

3.10.2 Resource allocation graphs

The state of a system can be represented by means of a system resource allocation graph. This represents threads and resource types as vertices. The edges represent requests and allocations. An example of such a graph for a system with three threads and three resource types, one of which has two instances, is given in Figure 3.20.

In this example, resource types are represented by rectangles, with individual instances shown by dots within the rectangle. Arrows from an instance of a resource to a thread indicate an allocation to that thread; arrows from a thread to a resource type represent a request. When the request is granted, the direction of the arrow is reversed.

If such a resource allocation graph does not have a cycle, then the system is not deadlocked.

Figure 3.20 A deadlock-free resource allocation graph

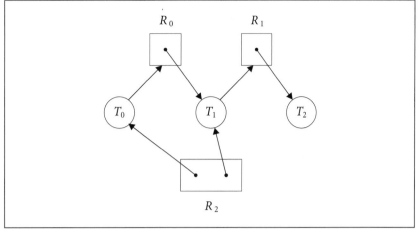

If there is a cycle, then it may be deadlocked, depending on the number of instances of the resources involved in the cycle.

For example, the graph shown in Figure 3.20 does not have a cycle. So the system it represents is not deadlocked.

If T_2 were to request an instance of R_2 then there would be two cycles, and the system would be well and truly deadlocked, as shown in Figure 3.21.

Figure 3.21 A deadlocked resource allocation graph

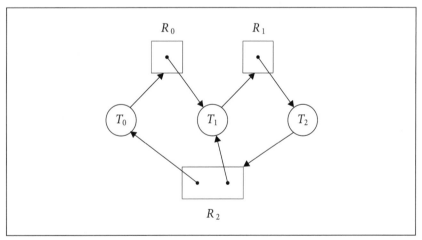

But note the version of the graph shown in Figure 3.22. There is certainly a cycle in the graph, but T_3 is not involved in it. T_3 is not waiting on any resource, so it is runnable. It is at least possible that it will return its instance of R_2, which could than be given to T_2, thus breaking the cycle. So we cannot say that the system is deadlocked. It may be; we just don't know.

3.10.3 Necessary and sufficient conditions

There are four conditions which must be true before a system is deadlocked. These are also sufficient conditions – once all four of them are true, the system is deadlocked, no ifs or buts about it.

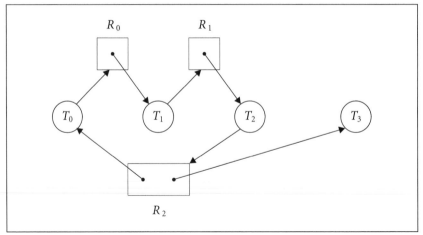

Figure 3.22 A resource allocation graph for four threads

These conditions are:

1   Mutual exclusion – the resources involved must be unshareable. Obviously if they are shareable they cannot cause deadlock, as a thread will never have to wait on such a resource.

2   Hold and wait – the system works in such a way that threads hold the resources they have while waiting for others.

3   No preemption – resources can only be released voluntarily by a thread: they cannot be taken back by the system.

4   Circular wait – the waiting threads can be arranged in order T_0, T_1, ..., T_n, such that T_x is waiting for the resource held by T_{x+1}, and T_n is waiting for the resource held by T_0. This is a generalized way of saying that there is a cycle in the resource allocation graph.

There are three possible approaches to the problem:

▶ Prevent deadlock by arranging that at least one of the conditions given above is not true. But this can be very restrictive.

▶ Avoid deadlock by checking each request for a resource, only granting it if there is no possibility of it causing deadlock. The overhead involved in this is so great that it is rarely used.

▶ Allow deadlock to occur, but be sure that it is detected as soon as it happens, and then try to recover from it. This is a suitable strategy when deadlock is very unlikely.

CHAPTER SUMMARY

▶ Operating system intervention is needed to control interactions between different threads running at the same time.

▶ Threads may need to cooperate to carry out some particular job. But they also may compete for exclusive use of resources. Both situations require a mechanism for threads to communicate between themselves.

Competition between threads can be summarized as the critical section problem. Each thread has a section of code, its critical section, and a solution must guarantee that only one thread can be executing code from its critical section at any given time.

Historically, solutions to the critical section problem were first implemented in software. But these algorithms all have the drawback that they rely on cooperation between programmers. There is no way to enforce them. So there is a need for operating system intervention in this area.

▶ A semaphore is a non-negative integer which can only be acted on by two uninterruptible operations.

WAIT decrements the value; if it is already 0, the calling thread is blocked.

SIGNAL wakes up a thread if there is one waiting; otherwise it increments the value.

▶ Semaphores can be used to control mutual exclusion (initialized to 1), synchronization (initialized to 0), and resource allocation (initialized to the number of instances available).

▶ A classic use of semaphores is to control producer and consumer threads, communicating through a shared buffer.

▶ Making WAIT and SIGNAL be uninterruptible requires some sort of locking mechanism in hardware, for example an exchange instruction. While this uses busy waiting, it is acceptable over the time-scale involved.

The implementation of semaphores also involves interacting with the scheduler, for blocking and unblocking threads, and managing the queue of waiting threads.

POSIX provides semaphores, which can be named or unnamed.

▶ Semaphores are not the ultimate solution to concurrency problems. They can be improved on, and there is also room for other mechanisms.

▶ Message passing mechanisms add features such as distinguishing between message boundaries and priority between messages. Such a mechanism can be synchronous or asynchronous.

POSIX provides a set of system calls for implementing message queues.

▶ A monitor consists of the data representing a shared object, which is accessible indirectly and exclusively through a set of publicly available procedures. The implementation ensures that only one thread is active in the monitor at any one time.

For synchronization, a mechanism known as a condition variable is provided. This allows a thread, under the protection of guaranteed exclusive access, to test some condition and to decide whether to block itself or not.

Monitors can be used to solve all of the classic concurrency problems, such as resource allocators, bounded buffer management and the readers/writers problem.

▶ The state of a system can be represented by a resource allocation graph. If there is a cycle in this graph, then the system is deadlocked.

There are three possible strategies which can be adopted in relation to deadlock: prevention, avoidance or detection and recovery.

FURTHER READING

Further material on interprocess communication is available in Silberschatz and Galvin Section 4.4; Nutt Sections 8.1, 8.2; Tanenbaum and Woodhull Section 2.2; Stallings Section 4.1; Tanenbaum (1992) Sections 2.2.1–2.2.4. The software algorithms referred to in this chapter can be found in Silberschatz and Galvin Sections 6.1–6.2 or Stallings Section 4.2.

All textbooks cover semaphores. See Silberschatz and Galvin Sections 6.4, 6.5; Nutt Section 8.3; Tanenbaum and Woodhull Section 2.2.5; Stallings Section 4.4; Tanenbaum (1992) Section 2.2.5. For more on hardware locks see Silberschatz and Galvin Section 6.3 or Stallings Section 4.3. Programming with semaphores is covered in Robbins and Robbins Chapter 8, Sections 10.1, 10.2; and in Gray Chapter 7.

For message passing, the theory can be found in Silberschatz and Galvin Section 4.6; Nutt Section 9.3; Tanenbaum and Woodhull Section 2.2.7; Stallings Section 4.6; Tanenbaum (1992) Section 2.2.8. Gray Chapter 6 covers the programming aspects.

Monitors are described in Silberschatz and Galvin Section 6.7; Nutt Section 9.2; Tanenbaum and Woodhull Section 2.2.6; Stallings Section 4.5; Tanenbaum (1992) Section 2.2.7. Robbins and Robbins Section 10.3 covers programming with condition variables.

For further reading on deadlock, see Silberschatz and Galvin Chapter 7; Nutt Chapter 10; Tanenbaum and Woodhull Section 3.3; Stallings Chapter 5; Tanenbaum (1992) Chapter 6.

SELF-TEST QUESTIONS

1 Give examples of situations in which threads may need to cooperate or compete.

2 Explain the semaphore mechanism and the WAIT and SIGNAL operations.

3 Give an example of how you would use a semaphore to ensure mutual exclusion, including the initial value.

4 Give an example of how you would use a semaphore to synchronize two threads, including the initial value.

5 Give an example of how you would use a semaphore to manage a set of resources, including the initial value.

6 Give an example of how you would use a semaphore to manage a bounded buffer.

7 Discuss ways to implement the indivisibility requirement of a semaphore.

8 Explain how the WAIT operation might be implemented within an operating system.

9 Explain how the SIGNAL operation might be implemented within an operating system.

10 Explain the difference between the POSIX named and unnamed semaphores.

11 List some reasons why semaphores are not the ultimate solution to concurrency problems.

12 Explain the message-passing mechanism, distinguishing between asynchronous and synchronous messaging.

13 Explain the basic idea of a monitor and how it is an improvement over other forms of concurrency control.

14 Explain the condition variable mechanism and the CWAIT and CSIGNAL operations.

15 Outline the structure of a monitor used for resource allocation.

16 Define deadlock.

17 Present the four necessary and sufficient conditions for deadlock to occur.

18 Outline the three possible approaches to the problem of deadlock.

DISCUSSION QUESTIONS

1 To insert an item into a singly linked list requires two pointers to be changed. Suppose a thread is context-switched out after changing the first but not the second. Draw a diagram of this situation. If the next thread to run now tries to traverse this same list, what will happen?

2 The C instruction `items--` compiles to the following code

```
ld items, r0
dec r0
st r0, items
```

The second instruction decrements register 0. What happens if a thread is context-switched out after the first instruction and another thread executes `items--` on the same variable? What happens if the context switch takes place after the second instruction?

3 One solution to the critical section problem would be to use a global variable. When set to 1, this means the critical section is occupied and no other thread can enter. When set to 0, it means the critical section is free. Each thread checks this in its prologue code; only if it is 0 does

it set it to 1 and enter the critical section. The epilogue code clears it back to 0.

Why will this not work?

4   Simulate the use of semaphores for one producer and one consumer with two people sitting across a table. A card with 0 on one side and 1 on the other can represent a semaphore. An enlarged copy of Figure 3.6 can represent the buffer. NextIn and NextOut can be simulated by index fingers.

You should find that no matter how the two threads interleave their actions, they cannot be putting into and taking out of the same slot in the buffer at the same time.

5   Reverse the order of the WAITs on SlotFree and Guard in the algorithm shown in Figure 3.9. Now run the two algorithms and see what happens.

Reverse the WAITs in Figure 3.10 and see what happens.

What effect does reversing the SIGNALs in either of these have?

6   How does the disabling of interrupts guarantee that a thread will not be context-switched out in the middle of a WAIT?

Why is it not an acceptable mechanism?

7   The provision of `sem_trywait()` in POSIX seems to be a great improvement – a thread need never block if it does not want to. Outline a situation in which a thread might still find itself blocked unwillingly.

8   POSIX message queues are asynchronous. Propose a set of system calls (including parameters) which would implement synchronous messaging. Add a broadcast facility to this.

9   Instead of blocking, a monitor could return a message saying 'busy – try again later'. Discuss the implementation of this.

10 Design an algorithm which checks for cycles in a resource allocation graph. What would decide when this algorithm is to run?

11 Suggest methods for preventing deadlock by negating one of the necessary conditions at a time.

12 Investigate the banker's algorithm for deadlock avoidance.

13 If a detection algorithm finds a system to be deadlocked, suggest some strategies for breaking that deadlock.

Memory manager

The aim of this chapter is to introduce you to the part of the operating system which manages memory.

After reading this chapter, you should:

▶ understand why a memory manager is needed, and what it is attempting to do

▶ understand the concept of virtual memory

▶ understand the four main mechanisms used to implement virtual memory – base/length registers, segmentation, paging, paged segmentation

▶ understand how memory extension works

▶ understand the reason for CPU caches, and how they work

▶ have been introduced to some of the classic memory management algorithms

4.1 Objectives of a memory manager

We will first of all look at the requirements of a memory manager – what it is all about and what it should do. When a C programmer thinks of a memory manager, the first thing that comes to mind is the `malloc()` library function. When some bytes of memory are required, it provides them; when no longer required, `free()` takes them back. We might appreciate that there is some bookkeeping involved in such a service, but not much.

This, however, is only one aspect of what a memory manager does – if the most obvious. There are other areas of equal, if not greater, importance. We will now look at each of these in turn.

4.1.1 Memory allocation

The hardware memory in a computer is linear, or one-dimensional. The range of addresses available goes from 0 up to some maximum. Programs are not written in this way. They are structured into procedures or functions, and each function is divided into a data area and a code area.

The allocation of memory should reflect this structure. The memory manager should not just give out one large block of memory, big enough to contain all of these segments. If the programmer sees them as separate units, the machine should too. So the memory manager must provide separate physical storage for each of them.

4.1.2 Multi-level storage

The situation is further complicated by economic and hardware factors. Memory is expensive. It is not as expensive now as it once was (in real terms), but it is still expensive. Programmers always want more memory, and faster memory, than is available. This has led to four-level systems, as illustrated in Figure 4.1.

Figure 4.1 The memory pyramid

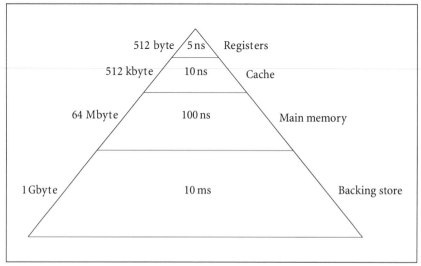

We are familiar with the idea of the executable version of a program existing permanently in a directory on a disk. This is normally a somewhat compressed version of the program. When that program is run, it is expanded to its full size, so that space is allocated for empty arrays and stacks. But it is not expanded into main memory – this is done on a special area of the disk, called the swap area or the swap file, or backing store. So while it is running, all of a program will exist on this backing store, or secondary memory. Such backing stores are typically of the order of 1 Gbyte in size and have an access time of around 10 ms. They are cheap, but slow.

About 10 per cent of the program will be in main memory. This will consist of the code and data that is currently in use or has been used very recently. Note that it is not 90% in backing store; it is all in backing store. The 10% is duplicated in main memory. Main memories are typically 64 Mbyte with an access time of less than 100 ns. They are faster than backing store but more expensive, and hence tend to be smaller.

About 1% of the program, the part currently in use, will also be copied into fast expensive memory, called cache. So this small piece of the program now exists in three places. Cache memories tend to be up to 512 kbyte in size, but their access times are around 10 ns. Again, we have faster but more expensive and smaller memory.

Finally, there will be one instruction and a few data items in the machine registers, the fastest, smallest and most expensive part of the pyramid.

Essentially, each level is compromising between speed and cost. But note that there will be up to four copies of some parts of a program's code or data. This greatly complicates the task of the memory manager. All of these copies have to be kept consistent. Also, organising the movement of data between the different levels of the pyramid is vital.

4.1.3   Address mapping

Only on the most primitive machines can you be sure that a program will be loaded into memory at exactly the same place each time it runs. In general, programmers cannot know in advance what other programs are in use.

So programs as compiled and saved to disk cannot have absolute memory references. For example, a program cannot assume that its variable X will be stored at location 1000. It cannot know in advance what location it will be stored at. It will be in a different place each time it is run. So how can it generate code to reference that variable if it does not know where it is?

One possibility would be to compile and link programs into executables as if they were going to be loaded into memory at location 0. So the compiler can be quite sure that its variable X is 1000 bytes (for example) from the beginning of the program. And it will always be exactly that far from the beginning. When a program is loaded into memory, a part of the operating system known as a relocating loader could adjust each memory reference to suit the particular location where it is loaded this time.

> For example, if variable X is 1000 bytes into the program, then an instruction to read X might be compiled as `ld 1000`. If at load time the memory manager finds a suitable free space at 2500, then the relocating loader will change that instruction to read `ld 3500`. And that is exactly where the variable X now is – 1000 bytes on from location 2500.

Such static relocation, which is done once each time a program is loaded, is fine for a single-user machine. But in a multi-user environment it begins to fray at the edges. Programs terminate, returning pieces of memory to the manager. So the manager finds itself owning many small segments, scattered around memory. There may be 1 Mbyte of memory free, but if it is in 100 blocks of 10 kbyte each it is not of much use. The solution is to compact memory, gathering the small unused bits together.

That means moving a program around in memory after its addresses have been adjusted by the loader. But it will not work in its new location. If the program from the example above is later moved to begin at 1200, the `ld 3500` instruction will now be looking at someone else's program. It certainly will not be looking at the variable X.

Because we have to accept that the region of memory allocated to a process may change during its lifetime, the memory manager must be able to change an address each time it is used, and in a way that is transparent to the process. This is called dynamic relocation, as opposed to static relocation.

4.1.4 Memory protection and sharing

At its simplest, this means that one user must not be able to trample on the space of another, or of the operating system. This interference can be accidental or it can be malicious. Protection involves both prevention and, when that fails, at least detection of the intrusion.

Every memory reference generated by a program must be checked at run time by the memory manager. This is almost impossible without hardware help. However, hardware memory protection is a standard on all computers nowadays.

But there are also times when more than one process *should* be allowed to access the same memory area. We have seen that cooperating processes rely heavily on this ability. So the memory manager has to allow this sharing without compromising on protection.

4.1.5 Memory extension

The physical address space, or the amount of memory actually installed, is limited by hardware and cost considerations, such as the bus width, the number of expansion slots available and the power supply.

The logical address space, or the size of a program, is limited by the number of address bits in an instruction.

This distinction between program addresses and physical memory addresses is critical.

On simple machines, the logical address space is less than, or in the limit equal to, the physical address space. But most modern memory managers allow the logical address space to be larger than the physical address space. They allow programs to run which are larger than the installed memory. And they allow many of these to run at the same time. How this bit of magic works is something we will have to study in some detail.

4.2 Virtual memory

We have seen that there are five basic functions which a memory manager must support. All of these are highly interdependent. Each solves a problem but introduces constraints for others.

In order for the memory manager to achieve all of these objectives, it is not sufficient for it just to allocate memory and then leave it. The manager must be involved in every memory access while the program is running. In this way it can implement protection and sharing. It can also maintain its multi-level storage system, checking whether the particular part of the program now being accessed is in memory or not. It can implement dynamic relocation, and memory extension, by using an address translation mechanism, or an address map, to change the addresses used by the programmer into the actual physical memory locations in hardware.

Figure 4.2 attempts to illustrate this situation. The left-hand side shows memory as it appears to a programmer. A program has a number of components, each of different size, and with differing protection and sharing attributes. The right-hand side shows physical memory, which is just an array of bytes. The memory manager sits in between, checking each logical address presented to it and translating it to a corresponding physical address.

Figure 4.2 Virtual memory

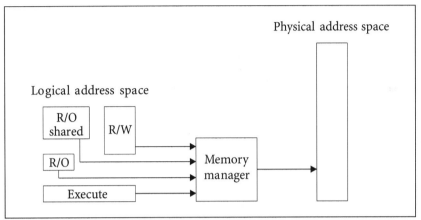

Such an address mapping allows a programmer to use a range of program addresses quite different from the range of memory locations available. For example, each of many programs can have a location 0, even though there is only one location 0 in physical memory. In effect, it produces a virtual memory, which is both convenient for the programmer and also achieves the objectives of the previous section. It transforms the computer into a more convenient virtual machine.

Various mechanisms have been developed over the years to implement such address mappings. We will look at the more common ones.

4.3 Base and length registers

This is the simplest method, so it is a good one to begin with. But it does not fulfil all of the requirements of a virtual memory; hence the need for the others.

With this scheme, when a program is compiled it is assumed to begin at location 0. And it is loaded into memory in this format – it is not relocated on the way in. As it is most unlikely that it will be loaded at location 0, this means that program addresses will be incorrect.

4.3.1 Relocation

When it is loaded, the address of where the beginning of the program is in memory is saved in a special CPU register, called the base register. On every memory access, the logical address provided by the program is added to the value in the base register to produce the correct memory address, which is then put out on the address bus (see Figure 4.3).

This has the advantage that, during execution, a program can be moved

Figure 4.3 Address modification in CPU

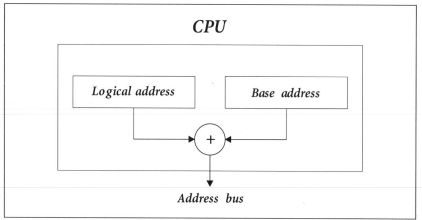

to a new location if required. For example, this may be needed for compaction. All that has to be done is to change the value in the base register. This movement is fully transparent to the user, who is totally unaware of it.

It is not economically feasible to have a base register for each thread in a multi-threaded system. So in practice the CPU has only one, which is loaded with the information for the current thread. When a thread is context-switched out, this value is saved as part of the volatile environment; the corresponding value for the incoming thread is restored to the hardware base register. This is the reason for a field entitled 'memory management registers' in the `volatile environment` of the `thread` structure.

4.3.2   Protection

With the scheme as outlined so far, a programmer could generate an address of any value. Hence a program could access memory way outside its own space. In order to protect memory, a second register is needed. This is called a limit register, or more commonly a length register. At load time, the number of bytes of memory allocated to the program is stored here.

Now when the program generates an address, the hardware not only adds that address to the value in the base register, but at the same time it also does two tests on the address. Is it positive? And is it less than the value in the length register? Only if both of these tests are true will the relocated address be put on the address bus. If either of them were false, it would imply that the programmer was attempting to access some information in memory either before or after the block allocated to the program. In either case the memory manager will give a memory violation error message (see Figure 4.4).

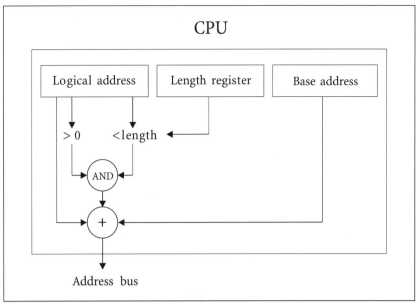

Figure 4.4 Protection and address modification

For example, let the value in the base register be 2000, and the length register contain 1000. This means that the program owns 1000 bytes of memory from 2000 to 2999. Now an instruction such as `ld -50` would be trying to read from physical location 1950 [2000 + (–50) = 1950], which is illegal. An instruction such as `st 1500` would be trying to write to location 3500 [2000 + 1500 = 3500], which is also illegal.

4.3.3 Evaluation

Base and length registers can be used to implement an address mapping. But this method still only provides one linear address space. Also, it does not allow the program to be larger than the physical memory. Memory is allocated in one big block. Protection is provided, but it is very coarse-grained. It covers the whole block of memory, and it either allows access or does not. It does not differentiate between different types of access, whether read, write or execute. It would be possible to share, but again at a very coarse-grained level.

So not all of the objectives are achieved.

4.4 Segmentation

What is needed to improve on the base/length mechanism just described is to allow a program to be treated by the memory manager as an arbitrarily large number of segments, not just one or two. It should be possible to give each of these different protection and to share them on a one-by-one basis. And there is still the wish to implement extended memory.

4.4.1   Implementation

The logical way to do this would be by implementing an arbitrarily large number of base/length register pairs in the CPU. But the arbitrary part is technically infeasible, and the large part is economically infeasible. So the solution adopted is to implement these registers in ordinary memory, as a table of base/length pairs. As each entry in such a table is controlling one segment in memory, it is generally known as a segment table. The entries are known as segment descriptors.

Instead of having a base and a length register, the CPU now has a register which points to the beginning of the segment table of the current process. The contents of this register are part of the volatile environment, and are changed at every context switch.

With this scheme, the compiler produces many segments of code and data, of varying size. Each segment corresponds to a function, or a collection of data. Each of these begins its logical addresses at 0. The linker binds them all together into one executable and gives each segment a unique number. This number is encoded in the high order part of every address. The low order part of an address is the offset within the segment (see Figure 4.5). For example, a logical address 4321 might be interpreted as byte 321 in segment 4.

Figure 4.5 A logical address

The segmentation mechanism has two functions:

▶ It performs the address mapping, which involves calculating the required segment number, and finding the corresponding segment. This is a hardware function.
▶ It transfers segments from secondary memory as required. This is a software function.

4.4.2   Address mapping

The hardware mapping consists of the followings steps, which should be read with reference to Figure 4.6.

▶ Break the memory reference into a segment number (**s**) and an offset within the segment (**o**).
▶ Use **s** to index into the segment table, find **b** (the base of this segment in physical memory) and **l** (the length of this segment).
▶ If **o** < 0 OR **o** > **l** then error.
▶ **b** + **o** is the required physical address.

Figure 4.6 Address translation
with segment table

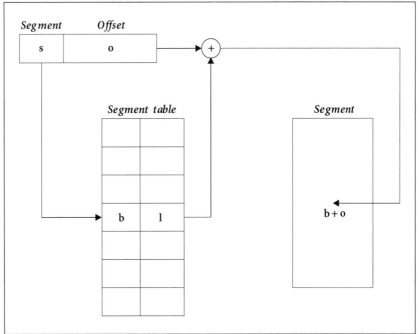

For example, take a logical address of 4321. This might break down to segment number 4 and offset 321. So we go to the fourth entry in the segment table. There we find the base address of the segment (say 12500) and its length (say 400). The offset (321) is not negative, nor is it greater than the length (400). So it passes both of the tests. It is then added to the base to give 12821. In this way, logical address 4321 is translated to physical address 12821.

Protection and sharing
Protection can be added to this scheme very easily. Three extra bits can be added to each segment descriptor in the table. When set, these bits signify read, write and execute access, respectively. Each descriptor in the table now has the format shown in Figure 4.7.

Figure 4.7 A segment table entry

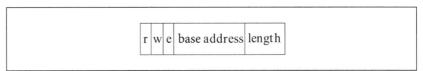

The mapping hardware can be extended to check these bits in parallel with the other operations. So there is no extra time involved. For example, a store operation would check if the write bit was set. If not, it would cause an exception.

The use of a segment table also facilitates sharing. First of all, because segments can be of any size, the programmer can indicate just which bytes of data or code are to be shared, and make these a segment on their own. Then each of the two (or more) sharing processes can have entries in their segment tables, pointing to the same physical location in memory. While the base and length part of the descriptors would be identical, it is not necessary for the protection bits to be the same for the two processes. If one process only ever writes to the shared segment, and the other only ever reads from it, then the protection in the segment descriptor of the first process would be set to write only, while only the read bit would be set in the descriptor of the second process.

4.4.3 Extending memory

Segmentation allows us to achieve another objective of good memory management – it allows us to extend memory. That is, the logical address space can be greater than the physical memory. We can write programs larger then the installed physical memory on the machine.

The essential point is that all the segments of the program are on backing store, on a part of the disk reserved for this called swap space. No matter how many segments there are in a program, at any given time it can be executing an instruction or using data from only one of them. So while in theory it may be sufficient to have only one segment in memory at a time, in practice it is certainly sufficient to have only a small number of segments in memory at any given time. Most commercial programs have large amounts of error-handling code, which may seldom or never be used. There is no point having this taking up valuable space in memory. Because only a fraction of the segments need be in memory at any time, the total size of the program can be much larger than the installed physical memory, and it can still run perfectly well.

To handle the mechanics of this, we need to add yet another bit to the segment descriptor, known as the presence (or valid) bit. This is set to 1 when the segment is in memory and the data in the base and limit fields is valid. When the corresponding segment is not in memory, this bit is cleared to 0. The hardware recognizes this bit and understands whether a segment is currently in memory or not.

Segment fault
When a program address refers to a segment not currently in main memory, as indicated by the presence bit being cleared to 0, a segment fault interrupt is generated. The current thread cannot continue, so it is marked blocked and put on a wait queue. The missing segment is loaded into memory and the corresponding segment descriptor is updated.

> How does the operating system know where to find the missing segment? When the segment table is first set up, at run time, it contains descriptors for all of the segments of the program, even if none of them is in memory. The presence bits are cleared to 0. The fields for base addresses and lengths are unused, so the operating system reuses them to contain the disk addresses of the respective segments. Then, when a segment fault occurs it knows where to find the appropriate segment on disk. It can load it in and then use the base and length fields for their proper purpose.

Placement policies

How does the operating system know where to put any incoming segment? It links together all of the free areas into what is commonly called a free list, or, as it contains all of the holes in memory, a hole list. Then bringing in a segment involves scanning this list for a hole large enough to hold the incoming segment. If no hole large enough exists it may be necessary to compact memory.

There are three principal algorithms.

Best fit The hole list is maintained in increasing order of size. The incoming segment is placed in the smallest hole in which it will fit. The idea here is that the unused fragment is kept as small as possible, thus reducing waste. But it is unlikely that it will be of use for anything else.

Worst fit The incoming segment, irrespective of its size, is placed in the largest available hole. The idea behind this strategy is that the resulting fragment will be as large as possible and will be useful for something else.

First fit The list is not maintained in order of size. It may be in address order or creation order, usually as a circular linked list, with a circulating pointer. The first area large enough is allocated. The next search begins where the last one finished. The idea behind this is that when the pointer eventually circulates back to the beginning so many segments will have been deallocated in the meantime that large free regions will have grown up there again.

4.4.4 Cache memory

The foregoing description of segmentation will work, and will achieve the objectives set out for memory managers. But it will be unacceptably slow. The time required for each memory reference is effectively doubled. The CPU has to read the segment descriptor, then calculate the real address, then read from that address. Even worse than that, segment faults slow the machine down by a factor of thousands. If they are frequent, even the fastest CPU will be dragged to a crawl.

We saw earlier in this section that it is not economically feasible to hold the whole of a segment table in fast CPU registers. But it is possible to hold some descriptors in the CPU at any time. So hardware designers generally provide a special small hardware memory, called by various names. It is most commonly called cache memory, but it is also known as associative memory or associative registers, content addressable memory, or a translation look-aside buffer. The basic idea is that the descriptors of the most recently accessed segments are saved, or cached, in the CPU, where they can be accessed almost instantaneously – certainly in less than 10 ns.

Associative registers

There is one fundamental problem with finding items in a cache. Because they are a random selection, they cannot be in sequential order. When looking for the descriptor for segment 4, for example, the CPU knows that it will always be at position 4 in the segment table. It is sufficient to use a construct such as segment_table[4] to refer to it.

Now the CPU cannot be sure that descriptor 1 will be at position 1 in the cache. And it certainly cannot presume that when it has found descriptor 1 in the cache descriptor 2 will be immediately after it. Descriptor 2 may be anywhere else in the cache. Or it may not be there at all. So addressing, or finding items in, a cache has to be done on a different basis from main memory. We have to store the number of each descriptor, as well as its contents. This is not necessary for a table, as it is implied by the position in the table.

Each cache register consists of two parts, a key and a value, as shown in Figure 4.8. The key is the number of the descriptor, e.g. 1, 4, 7. The value part is the actual contents of the segment descriptor.

Figure 4.8 Searching a segmentation cache

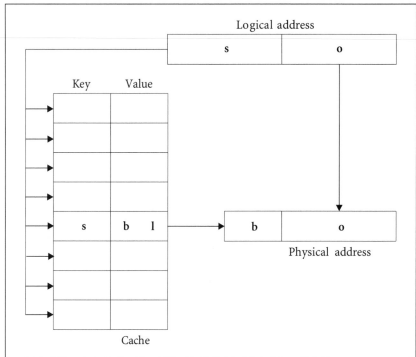

When associative registers are presented with an item, it is compared with all keys simultaneously. So if a reference is made to segment 4, all of the cache registers are checked in parallel to see if any of them has the key 4. If one has, then the CPU has access to the descriptor for segment 4. If none of them has a key of 4, this implies that segment 4 was not referenced recently. The CPU must then go to the segment table in main memory for the required information. When it is bringing it from memory it drops a copy in the cache, on the assumption that the program will probably reference segment 4 again soon. This adding an entry to the cache implies that some other entry must be discarded. For the sake of simplicity and speed, this is normally done FIFO.

It must be stressed that this is a very fast search, done in parallel on all cache registers at the same time. This makes for expensive hardware, and keeps cache size small. Translation buffers are typically around 8 kbyte.

> The cache is normally cleared on each context switch. The new thread will have segment numbers similar to the old thread, so unless it belongs to the same process it is necessary to clear the old entries to avoid confusion.

Instruction and data caches

There is a further complication, introduced to speed things up even more. Most modern machines have three different caches. One is the translation buffer we have just examined in some detail. Another one caches recent instructions that have been read in and executed. The third caches recent data items that have been accessed.

So after finding a translation cached in the translation buffer, the CPU does not always go immediately to main memory for the instruction or data. It first of all looks in the instruction or data cache. If it finds the item it is looking for, it does not have to go to main memory at all.

> For example, assuming a hit in both the translation and instruction cache, the effective time to read an instruction can be as low as 20 ns – much faster than direct memory access. But note that this speedup is due to caching – not to segmentation.

4.5 Paging

Now that we have developed such an efficient segmentation system, why is there a need to look further? There is still a problem with segmentation, namely the variable size of segments. This has its advantages, in that what the programmer defines as logical parts of the program are kept together by the memory manager. Protection can also be applied on a segment by segment basis. But there is the difficulty involved in finding space for a large incoming segment. Particularly when memory is almost full, it may have to be compacted fairly frequently. And this has a considerable overhead.

A mechanism called paging has been introduced to overcome this difficulty. The fundamental concept is that the virtual address space is divided into fixed size pages, not into variable sized segments. Physical memory is divided into page frames of the same fixed size. The size is not really important for an understanding of the mechanism. What matters is that on a particular system, all pages and all page frames are of the same size. So any page will fit – exactly – into any page frame. The problem of finding a place for an incoming page disappears.

As with segmentation, at any given time a process will have all of its pages in secondary memory and a few of its pages in main memory.

4.5.1 Address mapping

Let us first look at the address mapping function. The CPU presents the address it wishes to read or write to the memory management unit, which breaks it into two parts. The high order bits are interpreted as a page number, and the low order bits are interpreted as a byte offset within that page. The mapping, to find which page corresponds to this page number, is done using a page table, similar to a segment table. The page number is used to index into this page table, where the address of the appropriate page frame is found.

But as with segmentation, a translation cache is used as well. In Figure 4.9, the solid path shows what happens when there is a hit in the cache, and the dashed line shows what happens when there is a miss in the cache and the page table has to be used.

Figure 4.9 Address translation with cache and page table

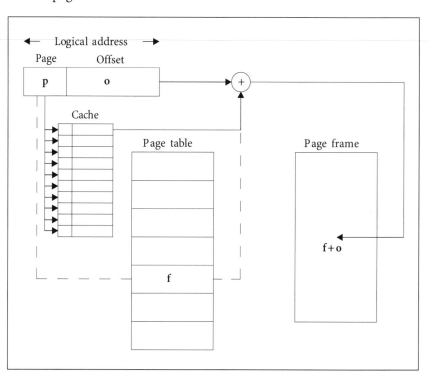

4.5.2 Page fault

When a program address refers to a page not currently in main memory, as indicated by the presence bit in the page table entry being cleared to 0, a page fault interrupt is generated. This is handled just like a segment fault, except that there is no problem deciding which page frame to use – any empty one will do.

If a free page frame is not available, then some pages must be removed to make space. The system would not wait until it had no page frames available – it would always keep a minimum number of free page frames.

Otherwise it might have no space in which to run the replacement algorithm, leading to deadlock.

4.5.3   Removal policies

The basic question here is: which page to remove? The ideal is to keep the page fault rate as low as possible, so the page should be chosen with this in mind. A number of different algorithms have been developed.

OPTimal
This algorithm can be stated very simply – replace the page which will not be used for the longest period of time. The problem with it is that it is impossible to implement, as it requires knowledge of the future.

But it is the best algorithm, hence the name optimal. It can be used as a standard against which to compare all others. We can rank an algorithm in terms of how close it comes to the optimal.

FIFO
This is the simplest page replacement algorithm. It can be implemented by allocating page frames sequentially and replacing pages in the same order. The problem with this algorithm is that it ignores the possibility that the oldest page may be the one most heavily referenced and be the one needed immediately.

A modified form of the FIFO algorithm is not to write the removed page out immediately, but to keep it on a temporary list which is written out *en bloc* at intervals. When a page fault occurs, the system searches this list before going to disk. This method provides protection against the relatively poor, but simple, FIFO algorithm. It gives a second chance.

Least Recently Used (LRU)
This algorithm uses the recent past as an approximation of the near future. It arranges all pages in order of use, and removes the one that was not used for the longest time. As an algorithm it is quite good. The major problem is how to implement it efficiently.

Not Recently Used (NRU)
Few machines provide the hardware necessary to implement LRU, but many provide some help in the form of a reference bit. At any time, the system can determine which pages have been used recently and which have not. We cannot know the order of use. Still, this allows the use of an algorithm which tries to approximate LRU, known as Not Recently Used, as given in Figure 4.10. The search is circular, and wraps around at the end of the page table. If a page has been referenced since the last time around, then it is not removed immediately. Instead, its reference bit is cleared and it is given another chance. Only if its reference bit is still clear when the algorithm has circled all the way around the page table will it be removed.

Figure 4.10 Algorithm for second
chance replacement

```
REPEAT
  Examine the reference bit in the page table entry
  for pagenumber
  IF (reference bit == 1) THEN
    reference bit = 0
  ELSE
    remove page
  ENDIF
  pagenumber = (pagenumber + 1) MOD size of page
  table
UNTIL (required number of pages removed)
```

Dirty pages

One other factor which influences page replacement algorithms is that there is a big difference between replacing a page that has been written to since it was brought in and one that has not. The former has to be copied out to disk, a time-consuming operation. The latter can just be discarded, written over, as the copy on disk is exactly the same as the copy in memory.

If we include yet another bit in the page table entry, the written bit, or the dirty bit, then any algorithm can tell these apart.

4.5.4   Page table organisation

Page tables can take up a large amount of main memory. Because the page table has to map the whole of the virtual address space, there could be very many empty entries. However, they have to be there as placeholders in the array of page descriptors. Techniques have been developed for handling such sparse arrays. One typical method is not to keep them in indexed order, but to access them by a hash function. There is a trade-off here between the size of the table and the time taken to access it. If indexed, the time taken to access any entry is fixed. If hashed, larger tables take longer. Another possibility is to page the page tables themselves.

4.6   Paged segmentation

Now that we have seen both segmentation and paging, a comparison of the two mechanisms should help in understanding both of them.

▶ Pages are of fixed size, segments vary.

▶ A programmer is aware of segmentation, not of paging.

▶ There is one linear address space with paging, whereas with segmentation there are many address spaces.

▶ Procedures and data can be distinguished and separately protected with segmentation, but not with paging.

▶ Sharing of procedures is facilitated with segmentation, but not with paging.

▷ There is automatic overflow from the end of one page to the next; there is no overflow from the end of a segment.

▷ When segments become very large, it can be quite difficult to find a block of memory big enough for them to fit in. A page will fit in any page frame.

▷ Segmentation was invented to allow programs to be broken up into logically independent address spaces, to aid sharing and protection, and to run larger programs without having to buy more physical memory. Paging delivers most of these advantages, but with a smaller overhead.

From this it is obvious that both segmentation and paging have their advantages, as well as their disadvantages. So some designers have implemented a paging scheme on top of a segmentation system. This is known as paged segmentation.

Each segment now consists of one or more pages. Each has its own page table. A segment descriptor now points to a page table. The hardware interprets an address as a triple (segment, page, offset), as illustrated in Figure 4.11.

Figure 4.11 An address interpreted as segment, page, offset

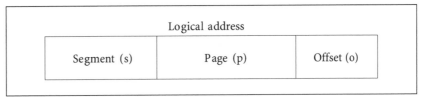

There is a considerable overhead in accessing the segment table and then the page table. The use of a cache is essential. The first time a page is accessed, a long and time-consuming address conversion is necessary, but subsequent accesses to the same page can be very rapid. The conversion of a virtual to a physical address is almost instantaneous if the page has been recently accessed.

Paged segmentation fulfils all the requirements of memory management. The only drawback is the complexity of the address map and the space overhead of the tables. But dedicated hardware, especially associative memory, can greatly reduce this.

4.7 System services for memory management

There are a number of POSIX system services which allow the user to interact with the memory manager.

It is possible to create a new segment in the virtual memory map and associate this area with a file on disk. So the file appears to be in memory, and is accessed using pointers, but in fact it is paged in and out by the memory manager, as required.

This has the advantage that it reduces the number of system calls which have to be made. With traditional file I/O, the operating system has to be called for every read or write to a file; this way there is only one system call to set up the new segment.

It also has the advantage that it unifies the data space of a program. Traditionally, a programmer has some data in variables in memory and some in files, with two totally different ways of accessing them. Mapping a file into virtual memory means that all the data is now accessed in the same way by a program.

The system service which does all of this is `mmap()`. It is also possible to lock a segment into memory and, of course, to unmap it.

POSIX also provides an `shm_open()` system service, which creates a segment of sharable memory. This can then be mapped into the address space of different processes, just like a file.

CHAPTER SUMMARY

▷ A memory manager has to do much more than just keep track of which bytes are in use, and which are free.

It must be able to divide up and manage memory in sections which correspond exactly to the divisions and sizes of any particular program. And it must be able to handle a three- or four-level hardware memory, maintain consistency, and organize the movement of data between different levels.

It is most unlikely that a program will be in the same physical location in memory each time it runs. Yet the memory manager must ensure that no matter where it is, all loads or stores in the program refer to the correct items of data.

It must protect one user from another, and yet at the same time allow them to share data and procedures when required.

Most modern memory managers cater for programs which are larger than the installed physical memory.

▷ All of these objectives can be met by making a sharp distinction between program addresses as seen by the programmer and the actual hardware memory locations in which the program is loaded. The memory manager uses a translation mechanism, or a mapping, to convert from one to the other, and so is said to implement a virtual memory system.

▷ The simplest way to implement a virtual memory is to use base and limit registers. The base register allows the program addresses to be adjusted on each memory reference, and the limit register implements protection.

▷ Segmentation provides an arbitrarily large number of base/limit pairs, but using a table in main memory rather than dedicated registers. Different types of protection (e.g. read, write, execute) can be provided. Sharing is possible by having a single segment referred to in the tables of two different processes.

Not all segments of a program need be in memory at a given time, so the total of the program can be much larger than installed physical memory. The memory manager needs to be able to recognize when a segment is not in memory and bring it in from backing store if required. Placement algorithms decide which free space to pick for an incoming segment. Common ones are best fit, worst fit or first fit. But fragmentation is always a problem.

Segmentation as described doubles the time required for each memory reference. It is made practicable by holding the most recently looked up descriptors in the CPU itself – in what is called a cache.

▶ The variable size of segments causes difficulties, which can be solved by paging. Programs are divided into fixed size pages, not into variable sized segments. Physical memory is divided into page frames, of the same size. So any page will fit – exactly – into any page frame.

Removal algorithms decide which page to remove in order to make room in main memory. Common policies are FIFO, least recently used and not recently used.

▶ Both segmentation and paging have their advantages and disadvantages. The best aspects of both systems can be combined by paging each segment.

▶ There are system services provided for mapping files into regions of virtual memory and for sharing regions of memory between processes.

FURTHER READING

The hardware aspects of memory management are dealt with by Silberschatz and Galvin Sections 2.3, 2.4; Nutt Section 4.3; Stallings Sections 1.5, 1.6. Silberschatz and Galvin have a section on protection, Section 2.5. All textbooks devote a chapter to memory management: Silberschatz and Galvin Chapter 8; Nutt Chapter 11; Tanenbaum and Woodhull Chapter 11; Stallings Chapter 6; Tanenbaum (1992) Chapter 3. For further information on the concept of Virtual Memory, see Silberschatz and Galvin Chapter 9, Section 21.6; Tanenbaum (1992) Section 7.3.2. Gray Chapter 8 deals with programming for shared memory.

SELF-TEST QUESTIONS

1 Explain why a memory manager is needed as part of an operating system and what it is attempting to do.

2 Explain what is meant by the term 'virtual memory'.

3 Explain how the base/length register mechanism implements the relocation and protection aspects of virtual memory.

4 Explain how address mapping is performed in a segmented memory management system.

5 Explain how memory extension is performed in a segmented memory management system.

6 Explain why cache memory is necessary with a segmented memory management system.

7 Explain how paging differs from segmentation.

8 Outline some of the policies which may be adopted when removing a page from memory.

9 Show how paged segmentation is an attempt to combine the best points of both segmentation and paging.

DISCUSSION QUESTIONS

1 If a program used only relative addressing, it would seem that it could be relocated without any difficulty. Why is this not a general solution to the address mapping problem?

2 On a particular architecture, the logical address is limited to 16 bits. This would seem to limit programs to 64 kbyte. Could you devise some way of writing larger programs, still with 16 bit addresses?

3 Do 'virtual memory' and 'extended memory' mean the same thing?

4 Without progressing to a full-blown segmentation system, could you suggest ways in which the base/limit mechanism could be improved? Consider areas such as more than one linear address space, fine-grained protection and sharing. How about extending memory?

5 The standard implementation of segmentation uses a segment table which is created by the compiler, so it is not possible to map extra segments in at run time. Could it be adapted for this?

6 A program generates an address 0xFDE9. The high-order 5 bits represent the segment number. Convert the address to binary and find the segment number.

The segment table entry for that segment says that the high-order bits of the base address for that segment are 0x213. Perform the address mapping and find the physical address.

7 When a process terminates, both its segment table and all of its segments actually in memory are released. Discuss the implications of this for a shared segment.

8 With memory extension schemes we can run programs larger than the installed physical memory. Is there any limit to this?

9 The memory manager can use a segment table entry for two purposes – sometimes it contains a segment descriptor, other times a disk address. But when it contains a segment descriptor the disk address is overwritten. How then does it know where to write the contents of the segment to when it has to swap it out?

Suggest an extension to the mechanism to cater for this.

10 When compacting memory, the simplest algorithm is to move everything to one end. But this may not be the most efficient way of doing it. Can you suggest something better?

11 As caches becomes larger, invalidating the cache on each context switch becomes more and more wasteful. Suggest an extension to the mechanism which would enable entries to be kept in the cache across context switches.

12 With a virtual memory system, two programs can have the same virtual address. Could they have the same physical address?

13 A FIFO page replacement algorithm can keep a temporary list of pages which are about to be swapped out, just in case one of them may be needed again almost immediately.
    Should a page on such a list have its presence bit set or not?

14 Investigate ways of implementing the LRU page removal algorithm and comment on their efficiency.

15 What is the essential difference between the second chance FIFO and the NRU page replacement algorithms? Both give a second chance.

16 It is far quicker to remove a clean page, as opposed to a dirty one. Evaluate a strategy which attempts to keep the maximum number of pages clean by writing back dirty pages when there is no other traffic on the disk channel.

17 If a page table is implemented as an array, it takes exactly one memory reference to access any element in it. If it is implemented as a hash table, what is the minimum number of memory references required to access an element? How large could this grow?

18 If a program is reading sequentially through data stored in a paged system, when it reaches the end of one page it automatically goes to the start of the next page.
    What happens when it reaches the end of the last page?
    If the data actually finishes half-way through the last page, what will happen if the program tries to read beyond the end of the data?

19 Could a page table be implemented as a tree structure? Discuss the implications.

20 Regions of the virtual address space mapped by mmap() are inherited across a fork(), but not an exec(). Why?

Learning Resources
Centre

Input and output

The aim of this chapter is to introduce you to input and output in an operating system. It concentrates on the high-level generic aspects, leaving the low-level details to the next chapter.

After reading this chapter, you should understand:

▶ the objectives of an I/O manager

▶ the distinction between the generic I/O subsystem and the device-specific drivers

▶ how I/O streams are recorded using human meaningful names, and how these are mapped onto physical devices or files

▶ the processing and data structures involved in opening a stream

▶ the high-level processing involved in reading or writing a stream

▶ the differences between synchronous and asynchronous I/O, and their respective advantages and disadvantages

▶ the concept of buffering and its advantages and disadvantages

5.1 Design objectives

Before getting into the fine details, it is a good idea to take a broad look at the area and lay out some of the objectives which should underlie the design of an input/output system.

5.1.1 Efficiency

Input/output is the classic bottleneck in computing, due to the enormous difference in speed between the CPU and memory on the one hand and the devices attached to the computer, such as a keyboard or printer. So there is great scope here for improving efficiency.

The twin aims are to have the CPU idling, waiting for a device, as little as possible; and to a lesser extent, to have all devices working as close to their maximum capacity as possible. We will see mechanisms such as buffering and direct memory access, which have been developed to help achieve these aims.

5.1.2 Device independence

The hardware interface to most devices is relatively crude. It requires complex setting and clearing of bits. The operating system hides these details. The user program sends a request to the operating system, which then does the required work.

Programs should also be independent of particular devices. It should be possible to request a printer or save a file without knowing the make of the printer or disk drive. If a system upgrades to a new model of printer or to a higher resolution monitor, programs should run as before.

A further aim is that the treatment of all devices, though they perform different functions and have different physical interfaces, should be as uniform as possible. So sending output to a screen, a printer or a disk drive should appear to a programmer as similar operations.

All of this is achieved by presenting the user with an interface which is as independent as possible of particular devices. As with memory management, we envisage a virtual device. The operating system then maps from this virtual device onto the real one.

5.1.3 Sharing

Many devices are shared resources. The operating system must be involved to allocate and protect them fairly.

5.1.4 Error handling

While errors can and do occur in all parts of a computer system, they are particularly common in the input/output area. There are two aspects to handling errors here: detection and correction (or recovery).

An operating system should be able to detect illegal requests, such as an attempt to read from an output device or write to an input device. It should also be able to recognize when data has been corrupted.

Sometimes an operating system is able to correct the error. Only when it cannot recover from an error does it report it to the application which requested the operation.

5.2 I/O subsystem

Figure 5.1 gives an overview of how I/O is dealt with in a computer system. User applications communicate with the outside world through the I/O subsystem using the system call interface. At this level, all of the possible different streams of input or output are treated identically. No distinction is made between terminals, disk-drives, printers and networks – or even between these physical devices and pseudo-devices, such as files or directories. All are seen as just sources of input or destinations for output. The programmer is presented with a consistent high-level view of all of the input/output streams.

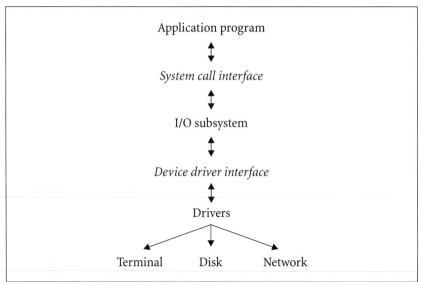

Figure 5.1 Overview of I/O processing

This abstract view is maintained in the I/O subsystem. All of the processing it does is device independent. It is particularly concerned with naming these streams, identifying them uniquely in the system and controlling access to them.

The I/O subsystem interacts with the device-specific layer, the drivers, through a standard interface. A device appears as a black box that supports this standard set of operations. Each device may implement these differently, but this is no concern of the I/O subsystem.

Device drivers are responsible for all direct interaction with devices. A driver consists of data structures and procedures, and it alone knows about the hardware characteristics of a device, such as the number of heads on a disk drive.

The remainder of this chapter will deal with the high-level I/O subsystem; the next chapter will deal with the low-level drivers.

5.3 Directory name space

I/O streams are almost always identified by human readable names. In many systems, a filename and a device name are very different things. Filenames are kept in file directories; device names are maintained in separate listings. Other systems make no distinction between the names of devices and the names of files; both are kept in the directory structure.

Unifying the file and device name-spaces has many advantages. Users are presented with a consistent view of the system. They can use their own descriptive names to refer to devices. The access control and protection mechanisms developed for the file system extend seamlessly to cover devices as well. For the remainder of this chapter, we will use the term 'file' to refer to any I/O stream.

To enable users to organize and keep track of all of their files, the file name-space is organized into a logical directory structure. A typical directory entry is shown in Figure 5.2. The type field specifies whether it is a regular file, a directory or a device. The location field contains information about the physical location of the file on disk or where the device is connected to the computer. It must be stressed that directories only contain information about files, particularly their names – directories do not contain the files themselves.

Figure 5.2 A typical directory entry

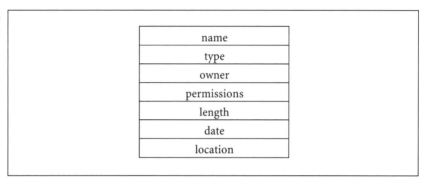

Such directories can be organized in various ways. The functionality provided by different directory systems is proportional to their complexity.

5.3.1 Single-level directory

This is the simplest possible organisation. All of the filenames are contained in the one directory. It would generally be implemented as a table, so there is a limit to the number of entries it can contain.

5.3.2 Tree-structured directories

This is a natural generalisation of the single-level directory and is illustrated in Figure 5.3. In this system, a directory (or subdirectory) contains filenames and/or subdirectories.

There is also a notion of a current or default directory. Users think of themselves as being 'in' a particular directory. It is better to think of it as shorthand – the system puts the default directory name before all filenames passed to it.

Most systems now treat directories as variable length files, each record being a directory entry. Information about a file, such as the name and where it is on disk, is kept in the actual directory itself. One field defines the entry as a subdirectory, a regular file or a device name.

The POSIX stat() system service can be used to read the information which the operating system maintains about a file.

5.3.3 Acyclic graph directories

The system shown in Figure 5.4 allows directories or files to be shared. We are not talking here about two copies of a single file. Rather, we have separate entries in two different directories, each pointing to the same

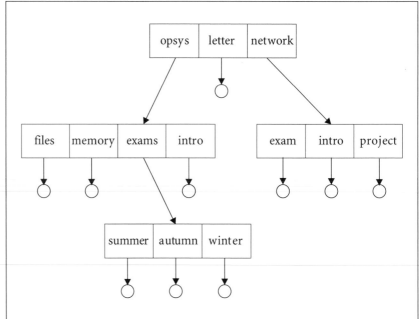

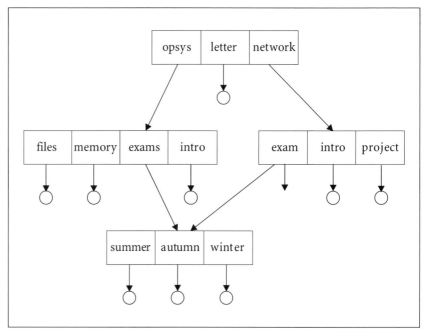

file. This can be useful, for example, to two programmers working on the same project. All of the project work can be in one directory, which is a subdirectory of both of their home directories.

The POSIX `link()` system call creates an additional directory entry for an existing file. There is no way to tell which is the original one. Remember that the name of the file is kept in the directory entry, not in the file itself. This means that a file with two links can have a different name in each of the directories.

> POSIX also has an `unlink()` function. This always removes a directory entry, but the space allocated to a shared file cannot be deallocated whenever anyone unlinks the file. Other users would be left with 'dangling' pointers to a non-existent file. One possibility is to keep a reference count of the number of users. When an individual user unlinks the file, this link count is decremented. When the reference count goes to 0, the data is actually deallocated.

5.4 Opening files

Now that we have looked at how sources of input and output are identified and recorded, we can go on to consider the processing involved in using them.

Before any source of I/O can be accessed, it must be opened. This operation need not necessarily be part of a source language. But it must be part of an operating system, which provides a system call such as `open(pathname, flags)`. The flags field would specify the type of access, e.g. read or write.

The essence of `open()` is to connect a user's program and its data. An overview of the operations required is as follows.

1   Look up the directory entry for the stream.
2   In the case of a file, if it does not exist already then create it (if the correct flags are specified).
3   Check the privileges of the user against the protection on the stream.
4   Check whether the stream is already open. If it is, then depending on the system it may just refuse access, or may refuse access if it is already open for writing, or may refuse write access if it is open for reading.
5   Create the appropriate data structures to represent this open stream, and link them into existing structures representing the process.
6   Provide the caller with some sort of handle to use for further operations on the stream.

Once a stream has been opened, it can remain open indefinitely. The operating system must remind itself that this stream is open and store some information about it. So it needs to allocate a data structure to hold this information. In practice this becomes a network of several data structures, as we shall see in this section.

5.4.1   Access and security

The question of security only arises when sharing is allowed. The owner of a file must specify which users have access to it and what kind of access they have.

There is a whole range of possible access permissions which a user may have to a file: no access, execute, read, append, update, change protection, delete. These could be arranged in a hierarchy, so that higher permissions imply all lower ones. If this were felt to be too loose, each possible access permission would have to be acquired individually.

To overcome the complexity inherent in controlling access for many different users, it is common practice to group users into classes, such as owner, group, world. Different protection can then be given for the different classes. But it may be difficult to decide who are in a group, and who are the world. There is also a problem with overlapping groups.

Typically protection information is recorded as a bitmap. For example, three classes of user, each with three possible types of access, can be coded in 9 bits, as in Figure 5.5.

Figure 5.5 A protection bitmap

Protection can be associated with the directory entry or with the file itself. In the former case, a file can have different access permissions in different directories. In the latter case, all sharers will have the same access.

5.4.2 File descriptors

The connection between the logical stream being opened in a program and the physical device is recorded in a stream descriptor list, or table. Each process has one of these, shared by all its threads. It is normally part of its task structure. One entry in this table is allocated each time a stream is opened. The entry is removed when that stream is closed. The descriptor is identified to the process by an integer, returned by the open() function, which is actually an index into the descriptor table. As each process has its own table of descriptors, the same numbers are reused in different processes. For future operations on the stream, the operating system uses the number of the descriptor to index into the descriptor table and hence locate the data structures associated with the open file.

Such a descriptor might represent a regular file, a device, or a network connection. But the file descriptor mechanism and the common set of I/O procedures which operate on such descriptors hide the distinctions between files and devices.

Three default streams are usually opened for each process: standard input (0), standard output (1) and standard error (2). Descriptor 0 is connected to the keyboard; descriptors 1 and 2 are connected to the screen.

5.4.3 Local file table

The system maintains an array of data structures known as the local file table. Each entry in this contains information relevant to one execution of the open() function. A file descriptor is essentially a pointer to an entry in the local file table. Figure 5.6 illustrates the connection between the descriptor table and the local file table.

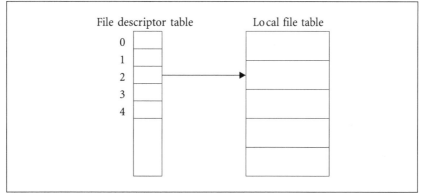

Figure 5.6 Descriptor and local file table

Figure 5.7 shows the contents of an entry in the local file table. The open mode flag indicates whether it is open for reading and/or writing. Probably the most important field is the offset into the file, which indicates where the next read or write will take place. The POSIX `lseek()` function adjusts this current file offset.

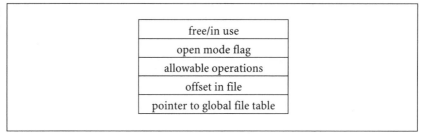

Figure 5.7 An entry in the local file table

5.4.4 Global file table

The information which an entry in the local file table contains about an open stream is specific to the particular process which has opened that stream. But there is much information about an open stream which is process independent. Inconsistencies that could result from having one file represented by two or more data structures are avoided by maintaining generic process-independent information about the file in a separate structure, the global file table.

Each active executable file, each current directory, each open data file and each open device has one, and only one, entry in this global file table. Each such entry is pointed to from one or more entries in the local file table; see Figure 5.8.

Figure 5.9 shows an entry in the global file table. It contains a count of how many entries in the local file table point to it and a semaphore to guarantee mutual exclusion on the entry. In the case of a regular file, it contains information about where the blocks of that file are on disk. If a stream is buffered (Section 5.7), then the global file table entry will point to the buffer.

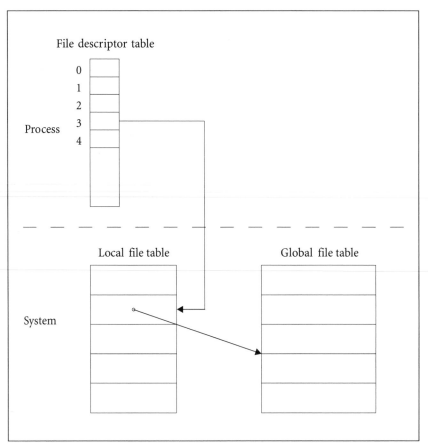

Figure 5.8 File opened by one user

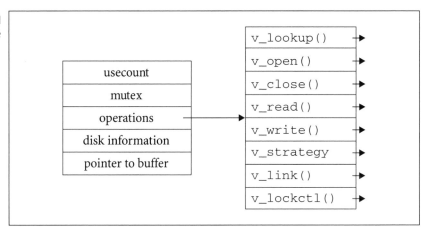

Figure 5.9 An entry in the global file table

Most importantly, it has a link to an array of pointers to functions which are specific to this particular file or device. These functions are provided by the driver for the file system or device. This is the point at which the generic approach begins to break down into file system or device-specific handling.

The function names are prefixed with v_ to distinguish them from the system services of the same name and to stress that they are providing a virtual interface to the file system or device.

The v_lookup() function is only relevant for a directory file. If the requested file does not exist in that directory it returns an error. Otherwise it either finds an existing entry in the global file table (if the file was already open) or creates a new one. The v_open() function is then called to perform file system or device specific operations. The v_close(), v_read() and v_write() functions are self-describing. The v_strategy() function is provided by some devices; for the moment we can understand it as a request to do input or output at some time in the future. The v_link() function is only relevant to directory files; its function has been described in Section 5.3.3. Finally v_lockctl() is used for locking part of a file.

We will look at implementations of these functions for file systems and devices in the next chapter.

5.4.5   File sharing

File sharing is possible on two levels. Entries in the file descriptor tables of two processes may point to the same entry in the local file table. This situation is the result of a fork(). They share the same value for the current offset.

Another possibility is that two file descriptors, in the same or different processes, each point to their own local file table entries. This is a result of two independent processes performing an open() on the same file. Because there are two entries in the local file table, each process can have its own different offset within the file. But there is only one entry in the global file table. Figure 5.10 illustrates this situation.

> With POSIX, system calls refer to files by giving a position in the file descriptor table. When two users share a file they both have their own file descriptor table. So one may refer to it by file-id 3, while another refers to it by file-id 5. They both have separate entries in the local file table, in which process-specific information is held, but there is only one entry in the global file table.

5.4.6   Summary

The whole procedure of opening a file is summarized in the form of an algorithm in Figure 5.11.

5.5   Input/output procedures

Opening a file is not an end in itself. It is done so that the file may then be used for input or for output. The subset of the system calls which perform these functions is known as the I/O procedures. These are the externally

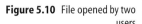

Figure 5.10 File opened by two users

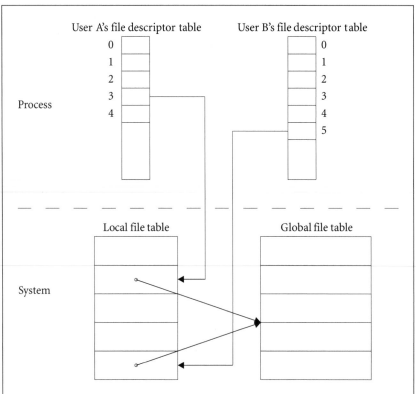

Figure 5.11 Algorithm for open

```
v_lookup()
IF not found THEN
  Return appropriate error code
ENDIF
v_open()
IF no permission THEN
  Return appropriate error code
ENDIF
Set up file descriptor and local file table entry
Link to global file table entry returned by
  v_lookup()
Increment usecount in global entry
Return file descriptor
```

visible interface to the input/output manager, called by the user process. They sit between the user and the kernel, checking and translating.

The following is an overview of what such an I/O procedure has to do.

1 Use the file descriptor number which was returned by open() to index into the file descriptor table of the calling process. If the descriptor is valid, the corresponding entry will contain a pointer to a local file table entry; otherwise it contains a NULL pointer and the request is invalid.

2   Examine the corresponding entry in the local file table and compare the parameters supplied by the user with those required or permissible for the device. Is this operation legitimate for this device? For example, a read operation on a printer is normally considered illegal. If the operation is not legal, return an error.

3   Pass the request on to the driver for that specific stream by calling the appropriate function (e.g. `v_read()`, `v_write()`) in the global file table entry.

4   When the data transfer has completed, notify the user process. In addition, for a read, pass the requested data back to the user process.

Figure 5.12 summarizes this in the form of an algorithm.

Figure 5.12 Generic algorithm for I/O procedure

```
Use stream number to index into the file descriptor
table
IF not assigned THEN
  Return appropriate error code
ENDIF
Follow the pointer from descriptor to local file
table
IF request not compatible with open mode THEN
  Return appropriate error code
ENDIF
Follow pointer to global file table
Call appropriate function
Return to caller.
```

POSIX has two main system services for I/O, `read()` and `write()`, each with three parameters: the stream number, the address of the source or destination of the data, and the number of bytes to transfer. Their functions are self-evident.

5.6 Synchronous and asynchronous I/O

There is always a delay with input or output. This can range from milliseconds for a disk drive to seconds or even hours for a keyboard.

In theory, the calling thread could continue with some other processing during this time. But that would not be practicable in most cases. With input, the data would not be valid. With output, the buffer could not be reused. So the thread must wait for confirmation that the operation has completed successfully. This waiting can be done in different places.

5.6.1   Blocking

One possibility, the one most commonly implemented, is for this wait to be within the operating system code, either in the I/O procedure or in the driver itself. The user thread is put to sleep, but the user does not see this.

It appears as though I/O is as atomic an operation as an assignment statement. This is known as synchronous or wait I/O.

This is the situation in a high-level language such as C. When a programmer writes a `printf()` or a `scanf()`, it is expected that when the program goes on to execute the next instruction, the I/O will have completed. It is also the default situation with system services such as `read()` or `write()`.

5.6.2 Non-blocking

This default can be changed to non-blocking I/O, for example by calling `open()` with the `O_NONBLOCK` flag. In this case, the `v_strategy()` function is called instead of `v_read()` or `v_write()` and all I/O requests will return immediately, whether they have been carried out or not. The actual read or write will be done by the driver in its own time. This is known as asynchronous or nowait I/O. The user must be aware that I/O is not instantaneous, and must not attempt to use data which has not yet been provided.

This introduces a requirement for synchronisation, and the responsibility for this rests completely with the programmer. For example, the thread could WAIT on a semaphore which the driver will SIGNAL.

Where the user thread does the synchronisation is important. It can come immediately after the call to `read()` or `write()`. This means that the user thread is suspended until the I/O completes. The effect is exactly the same as with blocking I/O.

It is also possible for the programmer to put the synchronisation further on in the code. In this case the program can perform other computations, even make other I/O requests, while the original request is being serviced. This method has the advantage that it leads to better overall utilisation of the computer system.

5.7 Buffering

The foregoing discussion of I/O procedures assumed that each I/O request from a thread caused a physical transfer to or from a peripheral. A thread which does a series of I/O operations on the same file, such as sequential writes, will be blocked each time it calls the I/O procedure. This means a context switch each time, which is a heavy overhead.

One solution is to perform input ahead of requests and to batch several output requests together into one physical transfer. This technique is known as buffering.

Data for output are accepted into a buffer at the request of a user program, e.g. a `write()`. The operating system then releases the data from the buffer to the device when the buffer is full or the device is able to accept it. The user has to wait only if the buffer is full.

Input data is accepted into the buffer from the device as rapidly as it can supply it. It is then provided to the user program on request. The user has to wait only if the buffer is empty.

Space for the buffer is allocated by the operating system when the file is opened. The buffer is pointed to from the entry in the global file table. Typically the `open()` command would fill the buffer. When the stream is closed, the buffer would be written out, if necessary, and the space returned.

5.7.1 Motivation

There is only one real advantage – improved performance. It reduces the elapsed time for a user's program by reducing the number of waits. This frees resources faster, so speeding up the whole system.

> For example, if it takes 30 ms to find a block on a disk and 3 ms to transfer it, that is an average transfer time of 33 ms per block. With buffering, two blocks can be transferred in 36 ms, or 18 ms per block.

But buffering cannot perform miracles. If the user's program supplies or needs more data than a device can handle over an extended period, then buffers are of no use.

> For example, if a data processing program is producing on average more than 100 characters per second and the printer is rated at 100 characters per second, then the only solution is to buy a faster printer.

When reading or writing random records, buffering can actually be detrimental to performance. Buffering would read in several consecutive records. It is most unlikely that any of these, other than the first, will be used.

> For example, if it takes 30 ms to find a block and 3 ms to transfer it, unbuffered this is 33 ms per block. If buffering reads two blocks at a time but only uses the first one, then the average is 36 ms per block.

5.7.2 Buffering algorithm

Buffering requires a variation in the I/O procedure. For example, an input stream handles requests from the user process by reading data from the buffer. Only when the buffer is empty does it call the device driver.

Figure 5.13 shows the latter part of an I/O procedure for buffered input. Most of the time the IF condition would be false, and the whole algorithm would be executed at memory speeds. It is only on the relatively rare occasions when the buffer is empty that the physical (slow) hardware is involved.

5.8 Locks

When many processes wish to open a file at the same time, some for reading, others for writing, there is the possibility of their interfering with

Figure 5.13 A buffered input procedure

```
Follow pointer to global file table
IF buffer_empty THEN
  Call device driver (for buffer-full)
  Process any errors
  Transfer block to buffer
ENDIF
Transfer data from buffer
Return to caller
```

each other. This is known as the readers/writers problem. An operating system can provide a locking mechanism which allows a process to lock either a whole file or part of it.

Such locking is implemented internally by the `v_lockctl()` function.

> POSIX provides locks over specified ranges of bytes in a file. These can be advisory, i.e. they do not enforce their use by other threads. One thread can find out whether others have a portion of a file locked or not, but it can ignore this information. They can also be mandatory, in which case the file system enforces them.
>
> It is possible to take out a read, write or read/write lock. Read locks can be shared, but write locks are exclusive.

5.9 Close

This function has to clean up after I/O operations. It calls the `v_close()` function in the global file table to do any file system or device-specific operations. For example, if opened for writing, a filled or partially filled buffer must be written out to the disk. If opened for read only, data buffers can be discarded.

It then deallocates the entry in the local file table and the file descriptor, and decrements the reference count in the global file table. If this is zero, then the entry can be released as well at this stage.

The operating system automatically closes all files when a process terminates.

CHAPTER SUMMARY

▷ Input/output is the classic bottleneck in computing, so an operating system tries to be as efficient as possible in this area. Because each piece of hardware is unique, the operating system presents the user with a consistent virtual device interface. It should also provide a comprehensive set of error routines.

▷ The set of system services that handle I/O make up the I/O subsystem, which takes care of device naming, access control, buffering and locking. It passes the request on to a device-specific driver which knows about the hardware characteristics of a device.

▷ Operating systems generally allow all sources of input and output to be referenced by user-defined names, so making the interface more user friendly.

Such filenames are stored in some form of directory structure. This may be as simple as one single table, but typically it has some form of tree structure, and may allow sharing, even under different names.

▷ The open() system call first checks if the file is already open; if not, it searches the directory structure. If the file does not exist, it may create it. It then checks the privileges of the user against the protection on the file.

When a file is opened, the system sets up a network of data structures in memory which are used for all further accesses to the file. Each process has a file descriptor table, which keeps track of all its open streams. Then there is a system-wide local file table which has one entry per open file per process. Finally, there is a system-wide global file table which has one entry per open file, no matter how many processes have it open.

▷ Input/output procedures sit between the user and the device drivers. In general, they check that the particular stream is open, and that the requested operation is legitimate for that stream. Then the request is passed on to a driver program for a specific device.

▷ There is always some delay with I/O, and there are two possible ways of dealing with this. The calling thread can be blocked, and the CPU given to another thread. This is the simplest approach, known as synchronous or wait I/O.

Another possibility is that the calling thread can continue with other work, but it has to detect when the I/O completes. This is known as asynchronous or nowait I/O.

▷ Buffering is a technique which attempts to batch together many small reads (or writes) into one larger physical transfer of data. It adds complexity, but is acceptable because of improved efficiency.

▷ POSIX provides locks over specified ranges of bytes in a file. These can be advisory or mandatory.

▷ When a stream is closed, the file descriptor entry is invalidated and the entry in the local file table released. If not shared, the global file table entry can also be freed.

FURTHER READING

General background on input and output can be found in Silberschatz and Galvin Sections 10.1, 12.3–12.5; Nutt Chapter 13; Tanenbaum (1992) Section 4.1. Directories are covered in Silberschatz and Galvin Section 10.3; Tanenbaum and Woodhull Sections 5.1, 5.2; Tanenbaum (1992) 4.2. On the programming side, Stevens Section 12.6 deals with file I/O.

SELF-TEST QUESTIONS

1 List, and briefly comment on, the objectives of an I/O manager.
2 Outline how the I/O subsystem fits into the overall view of a computer system, from the user to the hardware.
3 Explain how I/O streams can be kept track of using a directory structure. How is sharing implemented in this system?
4 Give an overview of the operations involved in opening an I/O stream.
5 An operating system keeps track of open I/O streams using three different data structures. Explain the reason for such a complex arrangement.
6 Two different processes are holding the same I/O stream open: one for reading at byte 100, another for writing at byte 200. Explain, with the aid of a diagram, how the operating system records this situation.
7 Explain the difference between synchronous and asynchronous I/O and their respective advantages and disadvantages.
8 Explain what is meant by buffering and its advantages and disadvantages.

DISCUSSION QUESTIONS

1 It is important to distinguish between information *about* a file (meta-data), and the information *in* the file. One possibility is to keep the meta-data in the directory entry. What other possibilities are there?
2 Could each thread in a process have a different default directory, or do they all have to share the same one?
3 An acyclic graph directory cannot have backward-pointing links. If this restriction is removed we have a general graph directory. Discuss the advantages and disadvantages of this.
4 How does the unlink() function know whether there is more than one link pointing to a file?
5 Read the manual page for stat() and outline how you would use it to build a directory listing program. There is one vital piece of information not given by stat(). What is it? Where would you get this?
6 Could each thread in a process have a different set of open files? What changes in the task and thread data structures would be required? What would be the advantages and disadvantages of this?
7 Instead of putting a pointer to the local file table entry in the file descriptor table and passing back an index into this table, it would be possible to pass back the pointer directly to the calling thread. Why do you think it is not done this way?

8   Suppose a program opens a file for writing and returns file descriptor 5. Investigate how you would use the POSIX dup2() system call to arrange that all output from the program now goes to the file and not to the screen.

9   The v_lookup() function searches a directory for a given filename and, if found, it creates an entry in the global file table for that file. This entry contains a pointer to the v_lookup() function. Do we have a chicken and egg situation here? How did the system know how to call v_lookup() before v_lookup() created the entry with its own address in it?

10 With the mechanisms as described, could two threads in the same process open the same file twice? Would there be one or two file descriptors? Would there be one or two entries in the local file table? Would there be one or two entries in the global file table?

11 In the algorithm in Figure 5.11, would it not seem more logical to check permissions before bothering about whether the file exists or not?

12 Distinguish between the POSIX open() system service and the internal function v_open().

13 What is the meaning of the value returned by the POSIX write() function?

14 Asynchronous or non-blocking I/O sounds complicated. Can you think of any real-life example where it would be worthwhile using it?

15 Should the information about buffers be kept in the local file table entry or in the global file table entry?

16 Some systems implement buffering not on a per stream basis, but on a system-wide basis. Outline some of the implications of this.

17 Rewrite the algorithm in Figure 5.13 for output.

18 Would information about locks be maintained in the local or global file table?

19 How does the operating system know which files to close when a process terminates?

Low-level I/O processing

The aim of this chapter is to introduce you to low-level aspects of I/O – the interface between software and hardware, control of devices and file systems.
  After reading this chapter, you should understand:

▶ how the software in a computer system interfaces with the hardware

▶ how device drivers are integrated into an operating system and the sort of functions they carry out

▶ how data is organized on a disk

▶ how the file manager stores and retrieves data

> In the previous chapter, we followed the generic processing of I/O down as far as the global file table. This chapter will consider how the set of functions made available there are actually implemented.

6.1 Interface with the hardware

First we will look at how the software of the operating system interfaces with the hardware. This interface is unique in that it does not – cannot – use the familiar function call/return mechanism. It is also very much dependent on the particular hardware involved. Here we will generalize as much as possible.
  This has always been one of the more difficult and unsatisfactory areas of operating systems programming, because I/O brings systems designers up against the real world. It is not possible to define interfaces to suit your own particular requirements – the interface provided by the hardware has to be used, whether it is suitable or not.

6.1.1 Simple interface

The memory in any computer has certain characteristics. First of all, each byte of it has a unique id-number, known as its address. Another characteristic of memory is that when we write some value to a particular byte, we expect that same value to be there when we read from that byte in the future. We expect it to remember that value – hence the name memory.

Memory may be visualized as dead-ended. When a CPU puts a value into a particular byte along the data bus, the only way that value can be read is along the same data bus, in the opposite direction. This is illustrated in Figure 6.1.

Figure 6.1 Computer memory

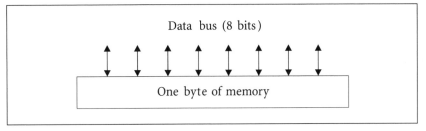

Device registers
It is possible to build memory so that it is dual ported. This means that there are two paths into and out of a particular byte. In such a situation, if a value is put into a particular byte there is no guarantee that it will be there at a later time. It may have been removed on the other path or rewritten over the other path.

This is the mechanism that is used to get bytes of information into and out of a computer. One particular location in the address space is chosen for a particular device, and instead of ordinary memory it is implemented with this dual-ported memory, more frequently referred to as a device register. One side of it is connected to the data bus of the computer, as usual. The other side is connected directly to the device. This is illustrated in Figure 6.2. Now the device can put data into that register, and the program can retrieve that data, as if reading it from memory. Conversely, the program can put data into the register, just as if writing to memory. The device can then read that data directly.

Figure 6.2 Dual-ported memory

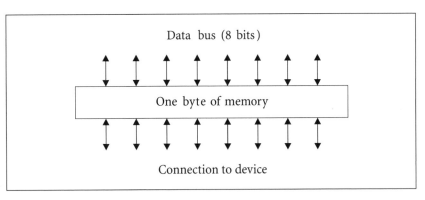

Synchronisation
But we have a problem with synchronisation. When a key is pressed on a keyboard, the keyboard hardware puts the value of the code corresponding to that key in the appropriate register. If the program does not remove that value before the next key is pressed, the previous value

will be overwritten and lost. Another possibility is that after a program has taken a value from the register, it may come back to take the next value before another key has been pressed. In this case it will get a second copy of the previous value, which is not what we want either.

So there must be some way for the device to tell the program that it has put in a value, and for the program to tell the device that it has taken one out and that the register is ready for the next one.

The simplest way to do this is to use another register. The first one is known as the data register, the second as the status register. Individual bits in this status register have particular meanings. For example, for an input device, bit 7 set might mean 'there is a byte in the register', so bit 7 clear would mean 'a byte has been read from the register'. With such a scheme, the device would check status bit 7 every time before it put a byte into the data register, and afterwards it would also set bit 7 of the status register. The program would first check status bit 7, and only if it were set would it remove the data byte. Then it would clear status bit 7.

Multiple devices

It is common for device registers to be implemented as separate electronic components, not physically part of main memory. Such registers still have their unique addresses, and are connected to the internal buses of the computer, as shown in Figure 6.3.

Figure 6.3 Keyboard interface with computer

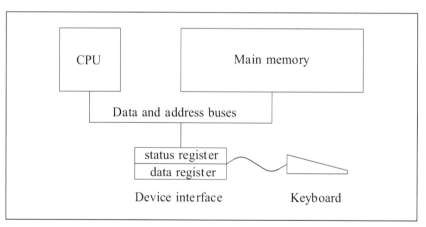

More complex devices would have more complex interfaces. A disk drive, for example, might have three registers to specify the surface, track and sector for the operation, along with bits in the status register to specify whether the operation was a read or a write – as well as the synchronisation bits and the data register.

On a realistic computer, there would be many such sets of registers. The CPU would periodically have to check the appropriate status bits for each one to see if it needed service. This is called polling. It is simple, but wasteful of CPU cycles.

6.1.2 Interrupt mechanism

Because polling is wasteful, another mechanism has been developed. A special signal line, called an interrupt line, connects each device with the CPU. By putting a signal on this line, any device can get the attention of the CPU. Such a configuration is shown in Figure 6.4.

Figure 6.4 Interface using interrupt line

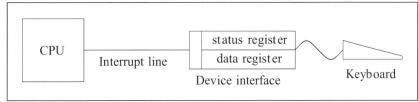

With this mechanism, the CPU can be busy processing and ignore the devices. When any device has data to deliver, it goes through the same procedure as before, but now it also puts an electrical pulse on the interrupt line. When the CPU receives this signal, it stops what it is doing and runs the polling routine. We still have polling, but now only when some device has data to transfer. We poll to find out which one.

The polling routine finds which device interrupted, and takes the byte of input data from it. The CPU then returns to whatever it was doing before the interrupt occurred.

How does the CPU get back to exactly where it was before the interrupt occurred? Presumably the CPU was executing an application program, unconnected with the source of the interrupt. When the device signalled, the CPU finished the instruction it was executing but did not go on to the next one. Instead, it performed a partial context switch. It saved the vital statistics of the program it was executing: the contents of the program counter (PC) and of the status register (PS). It then jumped to the polling routine by fetching its address into the PC register from a predefined location.

When the polling routine terminates, the CPU restores the saved values of the PS and PC registers, thus setting the machine up just as it was before the interrupt occurred. So the first instruction executed after the interrupt is the one that was about to be executed just before the interrupt occurred.

Interrupts are very frequent occurrences. The need to poll many devices each time to find the one that has actually interrupted is an unacceptable overhead. Hardware designers have developed the mechanism so that there is more than one interrupt line – 8, 16 or 32. Then, depending on which line the interrupt is signalled, the CPU automatically jumps to one of 32 handlers.

6.1.3 Direct memory access

All of the foregoing discussion, even with the most sophisticated interrupt mechanism, presupposes that data is transferred one byte at a time through a register. This is ideal for a byte at a time device, such as a keyboard. But disk drives want to transfer blocks of 8 kbyte at a time and network devices want to transfer 10 Mbit per second. In such cases it would be intolerable to have to interrupt after every byte.

So a totally different solution has been developed. The status register of our previous example is retained and even extended. The interrupt mechanism is also retained. There is no data register; instead, some extra processing ability is added to the device electronics. This arrangement is known as a direct memory access (DMA) controller and is illustrated in Figure 6.5.

Figure 6.5 Direct memory access

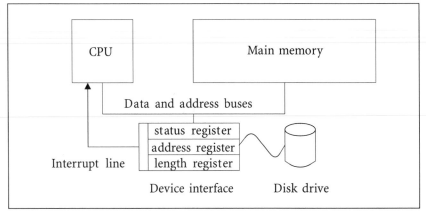

Let us now examine how an 8 kbyte block of data is written to a disk drive using DMA. The CPU sets up the various bits in the status register as before. But now the block of data to be written is not in a register – it is in the memory of the computer. So there are two extra registers in the device: one for the address in memory where the block is to be found and another for its length. Once this has been done, the CPU is finished and goes on to do some other work. The DMA processor now moves the data from main memory, sharing the address and data buses with the CPU. While the CPU is fetching an instruction from memory, the DMA controller stays idle. When the CPU is executing that instruction and not using the bus or memory, the DMA controller sneaks in and moves a byte from memory to the device. When the required number of bytes have been transferred, the controller interrupts the CPU to let it know.

6.2 Device drivers

Each physical device attached to a computer needs a program specially adapted to suit it, known as a device driver. This driver must be part of the operating system, or at least available to it, and there must be some standard way of calling it.

6.2.1 The device switch

The heart of the whole mechanism is an array called the device switch. Each driver has an entry in this array, which is filled in when the system is booted.

Each entry is a collection of pointers to functions. For each of these functions, the driver supplies an implementation specific to its device. The entry in the device switch is the only link between the driver code and the rest of the operating system. When a device is opened, the operations field in its entry in the global file table is set to point to its entry in the device switch (see Figure 6.6).

Figure 6.6 Global file table and device switch

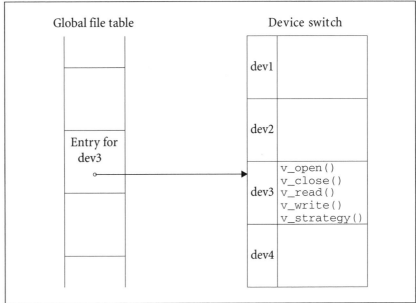

6.2.2 Input/output request block

Another data structure which is very important for a device driver is an input/output request block, or IORB. One of these is used to encapsulate all the parameters of each I/O request.

The sort of information contained in an IORB would be as follows:

▶ flags to indicate read or write, synchronous or asynchronous
▶ method of indicating completion (e.g. name of semaphore)
▶ location of data in memory
▶ number of bytes to transfer
▶ device number
▶ starting block number on device

6.2.3 Driver as a function

In some operating systems, such as Unix, when the currently executing thread wishes to do I/O it executes library code and then I/O procedure code, which calls device driver code, passing an IORB as a parameter. It is blocked somewhere in the driver, waiting on the device, and so is context-switched out. The processor is given to some other thread.

When the device is ready, it interrupts. The interrupt routine, running in interrupt context (stolen from the current thread), services the device. This part of a device driver is never called directly by a user, and usually has no relation to the currently running thread. It is not possible to predict when it will run; this depends on the device. It identifies which thread was waiting for this device, and moves it from the wait queue to the run queue. Eventually its turn will come, and it will wake up at exactly the point where it was blocked in the driver. It will return to the I/O procedure, to the system service, and ultimately to the user. Figure 6.7 illustrates this situation.

Figure 6.7 Calling a Unix-style driver

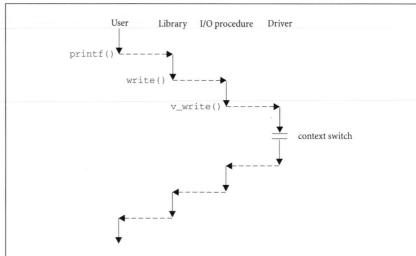

6.2.4   Driver as a process

Other operating systems take a different approach, and assign each device driver a process of its own. Such a driver process spends most of its time asleep. It is woken up when required by some form of interprocess communication. The simplest arrangement would be a message queue with the IORB in the message. Another possibility would be to have the driver process WAIT on a semaphore.

With such an arrangement, the driver code is broken into two parts. The first part is called by the I/O procedure as before and runs in the context of the calling thread. This code creates an IORB, and either passes it in a message, or puts it on a queue and does a SIGNAL on the semaphore. In either case, after passing the request on to the driver, the I/O procedure typically blocks itself until the driver notifies it that the request has been completed.

When the driver wakes up, it carries out the requested function, as specified by the IORB, and then puts itself to sleep again. When the device finally interrupts, it is the driver process which is woken up. When it has serviced the interrupt, it notifies the I/O procedure that the I/O request has completed and loops back to read from the message queue or WAIT on the semaphore again.

Figure 6.8 illustrates this situation.

Figure 6.8 Device driver as a
process

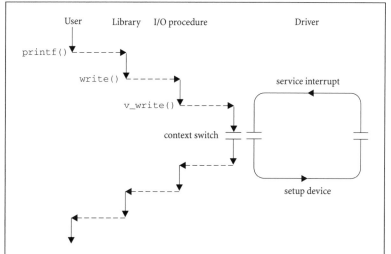

6.3 Operations on devices

We have seen that each driver provides its own implementation of each of
the functions which form the device driver interface. These functions are
usually written by the hardware engineers, who are familiar with the
complex requirements of the hardware. Here we will look at how the five
basic functions might be implemented in a very general way.

6.3.1 Open

While the processing which the v_open() function performs is obviously
very device-specific, it always has to check that the device is powered up
and online, i.e. that it is responding to commands. Then it resets the device
to a known state. For example, a printer driver might send an eject or page
feed command and move the print head to the extreme left position. This
guarantees that printing will begin at the top left-hand corner of a page.

6.3.2 Close

Typically, all the v_close() function does is to reset the device and
possibly put it offline. In the case of buffered output, it would write the
contents of the buffer to the device.

6.3.3 Read

The v_read() function implements synchronous read requests. All the
information relevant to the request is built into an IORB, which is one of
the parameters to v_read().

The algorithm for a driver which runs in user context is given in Figure 6.9.

Figure 6.9 Algorithm for reading from a character device

```
IF device busy THEN
   Sleep
ENDIF
Set up the I/O operation, as specified by IORB
Sleep
IF error THEN
   return value = errornumber
ELSE
   Transfer data to destination, as in IORB
   return value = success
ENDIF
Return (return value)
```

The following comments refer to this algorithm.

1   Normally a device can perform only one operation at a time. So there must be some way of ensuring mutual exclusion on the device. This could, for example, be a semaphore. Whatever mechanism is used, it must ensure that while a device is working for one thread any other thread that calls it will be blocked.

2   Setting up the operation involves writing to the control registers of the particular device.

3   The driver then has to wait, even if there are other requests pending, as the device can do only one thing at a time. So the calling thread is put to sleep. When the device has finished and generated a hardware interrupt, the interrupt routine will locate the waiting thread and mark it runnable. When it eventually runs, it will take up at the next instruction.

4   The test for error involves checking the status register of the device. The error number relevant to the condition is returned.

5   The data is read from the data register of the device.

6.3.4   Write

The processing for v_write(), which implements synchronous write requests, is very similar. An IORB is filled in, as before, pointing to the data to be written.

The algorithm for a driver which runs in user context is given in Figure 6.10. The comments made about the previous algorithm are also relevant here.

6.3.5   Strategy

The v_strategy() routine is a common entry point for asynchronous read and write requests. One of its parameters is an IORB.

If the driver code is executed in the context of the calling process, once the operation is set up, v_strategy() returns and the I/O procedure

Figure 6.10 Algorithm for writing to a character device

```
IF device busy THEN
   Sleep
ENDIF
Transfer data from user buffer, as given in IORB
Set up the device for writing
Sleep
IF error THEN
   return value = errornumber
ELSE
   return value = success
ENDIF
Return (return value)
```

can decide what to do next – either block or return to the user. Any other driver work is done by the interrupt routine.

If the driver itself is a process in its own right, then v_strategy() merely queues the request and returns. Typically the I/O procedure puts the calling thread to sleep at this stage; it is woken up by the driver when the operation has completed. The request is carried out by the driver in its own time.

6.4 Disk organisation

One device needs to be examined in greater detail – the disk drive. A disk is a collection of fixed size blocks. The block size is decided by the hardware designer. Current sizes are 2 kbyte to 8 kbyte. Blocks are numbered sequentially from 0 upwards and are always referenced by the driver in terms of this physical block number. Most of these blocks are used to hold directories and files. But there are also blocks used by the file manager itself.

There is no structure on a raw disk – it can be used with any operating system on any machine. A particular operating system imposes a structure on the disk when it formats it. Here we will look at how disks are formatted and how information is laid out on disk.

6.4.1 Boot block

The first block on a disk, block 0, is very special. It is known as the boot block. This contains the bootstrap program, which is run automatically when the machine is powered up and which loads and runs the operating system.

A disk can be formatted into many partitions, each containing a different file system (see Figure 6.11). So there is a standard disk label, also in the boot block, which specifies how the disk is divided up. It contains information about the hardware properties of the disk, where each partition begins and ends, and what type of file system is contained in it.

6.4.2 Allocation of blocks to files

We now move on to look at how disk space is used within any particular partition. The root directory is usually at some fixed position in the

Figure 6.11 Layout of a disk

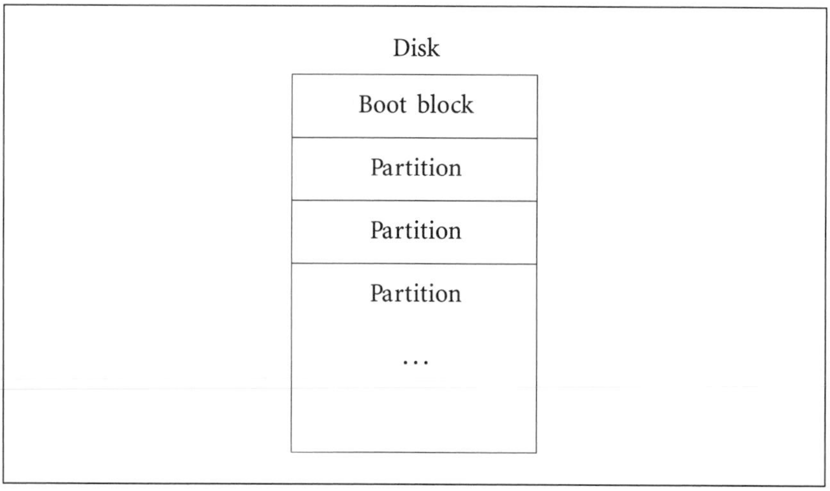

partition. This contains information about where all of the subdirectories or files contained in it are located. Subdirectories contain information about sub-subdirectories, and so on.

Different operating systems have developed different ways of allocating blocks to files so that disk space is used effectively and files can be accessed quickly.

Contiguous allocation
This requires each file to occupy a set of blocks that come one after the other on the disk. The directory entry holds the start address and the number of blocks. This method supports both sequential and direct access.

> For example, with contiguous allocation you know that block 7 will always be immediately after block 6 on the disk. Also, you can always calculate where block 7 is – it is always 7 blocks from the beginning of the file on the disk.

The difficulties are with finding space for a new file and with extending a file, as well as the need to compact the disk. Similar problems, and suggested solutions, have been seen when dealing with segmented memory management.

A variation on this used by most systems nowadays is to allocate disk space not in individual blocks, but a number of contiguous blocks at a time, known as extents or clusters.

Block linkage
Essentially the file is kept as a linked list. The directory entry points to the first block. Each block has a pointer to the next block. The last block allocated has a NULL pointer.

This form of organisation may be suitable for small files or for sequential files which are always read from beginning to end. But for relative files, to read block 17, for example, it would also be necessary to read each of the 16 blocks before it.

Even more seriously, if a block, or even a pointer, is lost or damaged, then the remainder of the list is lost. Not only that, but it may be linked into another file, or even into the list of free blocks.

File map

This is an attempt to improve on the foregoing, by bringing all the pointers for the whole disk together in one place. A map of the whole disk is maintained, with one entry for each block on the disk. So the seventh entry, for example, represents block 7. If the block is free, then this entry contains 0. Initially, on a newly formatted disk, all entries are 0. This map, or at least some portion of it, could be copied into main memory at boot time.

The directory points to the location in the file map representing the first block in the file. That entry contains either a pointer to the file map entry for the next block, or a NULL entry.

Figure 6.12 illustrates this. The only information about File A in the directory is the filename and the fact that it begins at block 1. This entry in the file map points to block 6, which points to block 9, which has a NULL pointer, signifying that it is the last block in the file. Similarly it can

Figure 6.12 Example of a file map

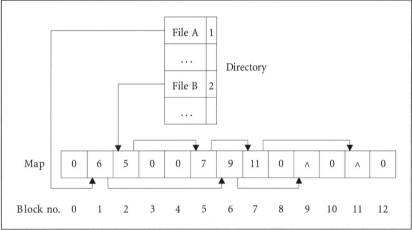

be seen that File B consists of blocks 2, 5, 7 and 11.

This has the same problems as the previous method, in that it is essentially sequential. But at least the sequential search is done in memory, at memory speed.

Indexed allocation

This improves on linked allocation by bringing all of the pointers for a file together into one location on the disk, the index block. Thus it makes the pointers contiguous. The directory points to the index block, which in turn points to a large number of data blocks, depending on the size of a block and the size of a pointer (see Figure 6.13).

This method supports direct access. For example, to find the seventh block you go directly to the seventh pointer. It also allows non-

Figure 6.13 Indexed allocation

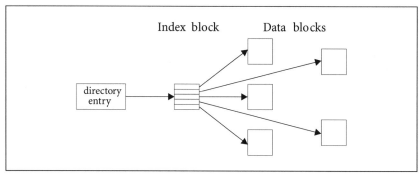

consecutive blocks to be written to a file without the need for dummy blocks in between as placeholders. The NULL entries in the index block are the placeholders.

A disadvantage is the small time overhead in reading the index block. Of course it puts all of the eggs in the one basket. If the index block is damaged, the whole file may become unreadable.

Evaluation
All of the methods described here have their advantages and disadvantages. It is possible to use more than one form of allocation. Unix, for example, uses a form of indexed allocation which is biased in favour of smaller files. For security, both index blocks and links could be used. As the directory is such an important feature in the whole structure this could be duplicated.

6.4.3   Management of free space

There are two possible approaches to this. All of the free blocks can be regarded as one large file. Or the free space can be tracked using a bitmap.

Free space as a file
One of the methods described earlier can be used to keep track of free blocks.

Contiguous A directory of free blocks is maintained. Generally, several contiguous blocks are allocated or freed at the same time. So free blocks are not tracked individually, but as clusters of free blocks. This directory would be maintained in size order. When allocating, policies such as best fit and worst fit are relevant. If a sufficiently large contiguous area of disk is not available compaction is necessary.

Links All of the free blocks on a disk are maintained as one linked list. Blocks can be added to or taken from either end of the chain.

File map Zero-valued entries in the file map indicate free blocks.

Indexed All of the free blocks are linked from one or more index blocks. The overhead involved in allocating or deallocating space is proportional to the number of blocks affected. But the addresses of a large number of free blocks can be found quickly.

Free space bitmap

Free space can be tracked by means of a bitmap, with one bit representing each block on the disk. The position of the bit within the map corresponds to the position of the block on the disk. If the bit has a value of 0 this means that it is free; 1 implies that it is in use. This bitmap is held on disk and loaded into main memory at boot time.

A bitmap has the advantage that it uses the minimum amount of space.

Disk space allocation strategies

The simplest approach to this is to use the first block on the free chain or in the bitmap. But a somewhat more sophisticated approach would be to use the block which will minimize the amount of disk head movement. In general, disk allocation policies tend to depend on the way in which free space is maintained.

There is some advantage in keeping all the blocks of a file on the same part of a disk. When allocating on a new disk, each file could be given a track of its own.

Blocks scattered all over the disk can greatly decrease performance. The solution is a periodic rebuild of the disk. This involves copying all of the data to another disk or to tape and reformatting the original disk. The data is then copied back in such a way that each file is contiguous on disk.

6.5 The file manager

The memory manager deals with storage, but only for the duration of a running process. At most it maintains information for as long as the machine is powered up. The file manager provides a facility for long-term storage, and is responsible for organising this data in such a way that the user can access it quickly and easily.

A file system is concerned with the physical properties of each file, such as where it is, and how long it is. Most files do not exist in their entirety in one place on the disk. Rather, they are scattered more or less at random among the blocks which make up the disk space. There is a parallel with the way pages are allocated at random to page frames. The allocation of files to blocks is a major function of the filing system.

The function pointers in a global file table entry representing a regular file do not point to the device switch entry for the driver of the disk drive on which the file is stored. Rather, they point to the code of the file manager. We will now look at how these functions are implemented within the file manager.

6.5.1 Open

By the time the v_open() function is called, the open() I/O procedure has already set up an entry in the global file table. This function is mainly concerned with access checks. The rights of a process have to be compared with the protection attributes of the file.

If this test is passed, the function reads information from the disk about the allocation of the file. This might be as simple as a pointer, either to the first disk block or to the first entry in the file map, or it might be a whole index block. This information is then saved in the global file table entry.

6.5.2 Close

The v_close() function merely flushes any dirty pages it may have buffered, and updates the information in the directory entry, e.g. the date field and possibly the length field.

6.5.3 Read

The v_read() function uses the information from the global file table about where the file is on disk, to calculate a physical block number for the section of the file it is requested to read. It then passes a request for that block on to the device driver for the disk on which the file is stored.

> For example, suppose v_read() is asked for 100 bytes, beginning at offset 1400. If the page size is 512 bytes, then dividing 1400 by 512 gives 2, with a remainder of 376. So it wants 100 bytes from block 2 of the file, beginning at byte 376 in that block.
>
> It uses the information in the global file table to convert logical block 2 in this file to a physical block number on the disk, and then asks the disk driver for that block.
>
> It extracts the required sequence of bytes from that block and sends them back to the I/O procedure for eventual transmission to the user.

For reasons of efficiency, it will keep a copy of this block, as some other part of it is likely to be needed again in the near future. This is known as buffering or caching disk blocks. It is similar in intention to the CPU cache, but should not be confused with it. For one thing, it is not associative.

6.5.4 Write

The v_write() function is very similar in operation to v_read(). If the block is already buffered in memory it will make the changes there. Otherwise it will first read in the whole block, then change the specified bytes. In any case, it will wait until it has a full block written in memory; then it will call the disk driver to copy it back to the disk.

CHAPTER SUMMARY

▶ The interface between the operating system and the hardware is implemented by means of dual-ported memory known as device registers. Data can be moved in or out through such registers one byte at a time.

  To avoid the CPU wasting time repeatedly checking to see if there is new data available, an interrupt mechanism can be added.

Finally, peripheral processing units known as DMA controllers can be used to handle all the work of moving data between memory and a device, leaving the CPU free for more productive processing.

▶ Each configured device has an entry in the device switch containing pointers to device-specific functions. These are implemented by a device driver, a part of the operating system that is specially tailored to each individual piece of hardware.

▶ Each driver provides its own implementation of the functions which form the device driver interface. The `v_read()` and `v_write()` functions are synchronous, while `v_strategy()` is asynchronous.

▶ Some of the space on each disk is used for administrative purposes. This includes the disk label and the boot block.

Various schemes are used for allocating blocks to files. One possibility is that a file is kept in contiguous blocks. Another possibility is that the blocks of a given file are linked together by pointers, much like a linked list. Two improvements on that are to bring all the pointers for the whole disk together in a file map, or to bring all the pointers for a particular file together in an index block.

All free blocks on a disk can be treated as one large file. Another possibility is to track blocks as free or in use by means of a bitmap.

▶ The file manager provides a facility for long-term storage. The virtual interface in the global file table specifies a standard set of operations on files, and each file system type is expected to provide its own implementation of these.

FURTHER READING

General background on devices can be found in Silberschatz and Galvin Sections 2.2, 12.2; Nutt Chapter 5; Stallings Chapter 10; Tanenbaum (1992) Chapter 5. Nutt Section 4.4 introduces device hardware. Interrupt handling is described in Nutt Section 4.5; Stallings Section 1.4.

Disk organisation is described in Silberschatz and Galvin Chapter 13; Stallings Section 11.6. File organisation is covered by Silberschatz and Galvin Chapter 11; Tanenbaum and Woodhull Section 5.3; Tanenbaum (1992) Section 4.3. Robbins and Robbins covers file-related system services in Chapter 3.

SELF-TEST QUESTIONS

1 Explain how data is moved in and out of a computer using device registers.

2 Explain how interrupt-driven I/O works and the advantage of it.

3 Explain what is meant by DMA and the advantage of it.

> 4 Device drivers can be implemented as functions which run in the context of the calling thread, or they can be implemented as operating system threads in their own right. Explain the two arrangements and mention advantages and disadvantages.
>
> 5 Give an overview of how a device driver might implement the five major functions open, close, read, write, strategy.
>
> 6 Outline four methods of allocating disk blocks to files, comparing the advantages and disadvantages.
>
> 7 Give an overview of how a file manager might implement the four major operations open, close, read, write.

DISCUSSION QUESTIONS

1 When a device interrupts, the PC and PS of the running thread are stored automatically and the PC and PS of the interrupt handler loaded into the hardware registers. But the general-purpose registers still contain values belonging to the running thread – there has not been a full context switch.

   The interrupt handler cannot run without using some general-purpose registers. How can it do this without overwriting values belonging to the running thread?

2 When a device is opened, the operations field in its entry in the global file table is set to point to its entry in the device switch. How can the system know *which* entry in the device switch corresponds to the device it is opening?

3 Compare the advantages and disadvantages of running a device driver in the context of the calling thread or making it a process in its own right.

4 Rewrite the algorithms in Figure 6.9 and 6.10 for a driver which is implemented as a process in its own right.

5 It is a common problem that disks formatted by one operating system cannot be read by any other. Would a common disk label (across all operating systems) help?

6 In a system using contiguous allocation, a file contains 10 blocks. Explain what is involved in adding a block (a) at the beginning, (b) in the middle and (c) at the end.

7 Repeat Question 6 for block linkage, file map and indexed allocation.

8 Block linkage is very susceptible to damaged pointers. Could you suggest any extensions which would make it possible to reconstruct files, even if one or more pointers were lost?

9 Explain how indexed allocation allows for holes in files, e.g. it is possible to have record 1 and record 10 000 without allocating space for the intervening records.

10 When compaction is required in a contiguous allocation scheme, is it necessary to compact the whole disk, or would it be sufficient to compact each track? Is there any time difference?

11 Both a bitmap and a file map use a map of the disk. What is the essential difference between them?

12 When using a bitmap to keep track of free space, it is important to maintain consistency between the directory and the bitmap. Which should be updated first?

13 When the file manager has calculated a physical block number, how does it ask the disk driver to read that block?

Distributed systems

CHAPTER OVERVIEW

The aim of this chapter is to introduce you to distributed computer systems, including communication mechanisms and various services which can be built on top of these.

Having read this chapter, you should understand:

▶ the features specific to distributed systems

▶ the mechanism used for naming resources in such systems

▶ different paradigms used in designing and building such systems, including CORBA and DCE

▶ the communication mechanisms upon which distributed systems can be built, particularly sockets and RPC

▶ distributed services, such as mutual exclusion, deadlock detection, shared memory and file systems

7.1 Introduction

Computer systems have developed from standalone machines, to direct connections between two machines, to networks where one machine can communicate with any other networked machine. But even with this, the user is always aware of the connection and has to issue explicit commands for the movement of data.

Now we are on the verge of the next development, building on networking. This involves groups of machines acting together as one. A distributed system is a collection of individual computers which are networked together not just to share data, but to cooperate, to distribute computation among several physical machines.

Distribution must be transparent, both to the user and to programs at the system call interface. This means that the user or programmer should not be able to tell that a remote machine is involved. Ideally, a distributed system should look like a conventional system to users. Software for this is just emerging.

The simplest possible architecture used to structure a distributed system is to arrange for some processes to provide services to others. Those which provide services are known as servers, naturally enough. Those which use these services are known as clients. The whole arrangement is known as a client/server system. What the server does, and what it sends back to the client (if anything) can vary enormously. But all of the different models of distributed computing can be reduced to this.

7.2 Features of distributed systems

Distributed systems have some features not found in standalone systems, and these are influencing the pace of development.

7.2.1 Economy

Probably the single most important argument for the move towards distributing computing resources is the economic one. At present the ratio between price and performance is in favour of multiple small machines. A microcomputer can only provide limited performance; but if microcomputers can be added together to provide a cumulative performance, they will do so at a fraction of the cost of a mainframe.

Sharing the workload over idle workstations is one of the long-term goals of distributed systems. The ideal here is that when a personal workstation is idle, it would make itself available and undertake work for other, busier, machines. But it would always be fully available for its owner when required.

7.2.2 Reliability

Distributed systems can offer the high reliability and fault tolerance needed by critical applications. This is achieved by redundancy in processing power, other hardware and storage of data. If one machine in a group of 10 crashes, 90% of the processing power is still available. One copy of a database may be destroyed, but with proper systems in place it can be ensured that other up-to-date copies exist and are immediately available. The user need not even be aware that there was a problem.

7.2.3 Resource sharing

This is another factor driving the development of distributed systems. Such sharing can be for purely economic reasons, for example to use an expensive printer or other specialized hardware. A multi-user licence for one shared copy of a piece of software is cheaper than many single-user licences.

Apart from economic reasons, it can often be very convenient to share resources. It is not really feasible to share a company's database by distributing copies on floppy disks to individual machines – it would never be up to date! The whole area of computer-supported cooperative work relies heavily on distributed systems.

7.2.4 Performance

Obviously performance can be improved by using more machines. But there is a downside. Communication is the great bottleneck here. So processes and the resources they use should still be on the same machine as much as possible. Another critical factor is the ability to adapt to increased load. The system should not just collapse under load. Performance should degrade gracefully.

7.2.5 Incremental growth

Distributed systems allow for the incremental growth of a computer installation. It is not necessary to buy all the processing power, memory or disk drives at the one time. It is possible to install just what is necessary to begin with, knowing that the system can expand to keep pace with growing demand into the foreseeable future.

7.3 Naming

In a distributed system, it is necessary to be able to identify uniquely all of the resources – individual machines, processes, files, printers. At the system level, these identifiers are binary numbers. There are two problems with such identifiers.

One is that humans find such binary numbers, or even their decimal equivalents, difficult to remember and input. We are much more at home with names.

The second problem is even more serious. A client needs to know the identifier of the server machine and also the identifier of the process on that machine which is providing the required service. Suppose this server process crashes and restarts. It will now have a different process id, and clients will not be able to reach it. Another possibility is that the machine itself may crash and the system administrator may move the server process to another machine. Clients would continue sending requests to the old server, with no results.

7.3.1 Name server

There is one solution to both of these problems, and that is to provide a name server in the system. At the human level, resources are identified by meaningful names, such as 'timeserver' or 'laserprinter'. At the machine level they are still identified by binary numbers. The link between a name and a number is called a binding. Then we add in a name server process, somewhere in the system. This maintains a database of such bindings and performs translations on behalf of clients. For example, a process sends the name server the string 'laserprinter', and it sends back the unique identifier of that printer. If the identifier changes, it is only necessary to inform the name server. As long as a process can find the name server, it can find any other resources in the system.

7.3.2 Internet names and addresses

Each computer attached to the Internet is known by a name and also by a number.

Internet naming convention
All of the names given to computers on the Internet are arranged in a tree
structure, just like the directory structure of a file system. Each non-leaf
node in this tree is known as a domain.

> Names can be relative (to the local domain), or they can be absolute. Absolute
> names always terminate with a dot.

There is a root, then first-level domains, such as `com`, `org` and `edu`.
There are also first-level domains for individual countries, such as `us` and
`ie` etc. Each of these domains is divided into subdomains, and so on.
Figure 7.1 gives an example of a tiny fraction of the namespace. A typical
name for a computer attached to the Internet would be
`shannon.cs.ul.ie`.

Figure 7.1 Part of the Internet
domain name space

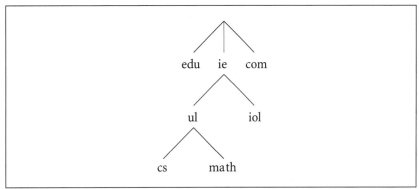

Internet protocol address
While we are familiar with these human-readable names, we must
remember that the Internet works with binary addresses. All of the data
passing around the Internet is directed to its destination by means of
these numeric addresses. Such Internet protocol (IP) addresses are 32 bit
integers. When humans deal with them, we usually break them into four
bytes and write the decimal equivalent of each byte separated by a dot,
e.g. `136.201.24.2`. This is known as dotted decimal format.

7.3.3 Internet name server

The Internet domain name system (DNS) is the system which keeps track
of all of the computers attached to the Internet. Its role is to translate a
name such as `shannon.cs.ul.ie` into an IP address, such as
`136.201.24.2`.

Figure 7.2 illustrates the procedure. A client knows the name of a
server. But in order to send a request to that server, it must know its
address. So it first sends a request to the name server, asking it to

Figure 7.2 Using a name server

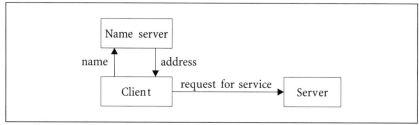

translate the name to an address. The name server looks up the required address in its database and sends it back to the client. The client is then able to send a request for service.

Distributed database

Having one name server to cater for the whole of the Internet just would not work. So the designers came up with the idea of breaking up the overall database of name/number pairs, and keeping parts of it on many different machines around the world. This may seem to make the problem even worse, but in fact it is a very elegant solution, as we shall see.

Each domain of the Internet has an administrator who undertakes to assign names and numbers to machines in that domain. The administrator also undertakes to provide a name translation server for that domain.

To tie the whole system together, there are a number of root servers in different parts of the world which know the addresses of the servers for all of the first-level domains – `org`, `com`, `us`, `ie` etc. All servers the world over have the addresses of these root servers.

If a name server is presented with a name in its own domain, then it can give a reply immediately. However, if the name is in some other domain, then there are further steps involved. For example, a server presented with the name `shannon.cs.ul.ie` will first of all query a root server for the address of the name server for the `ie` domain. Then it will query that server for the address of the name server for the `ul.ie` domain. Then it will query that server for the address of the name server for the `cs.ul.ie` domain. Finally it will query that server for the address of the machine `shannon`. Like a good librarian, the server may not have some particular information, but it must know where to look for it.

The full procedure is outlined in Figure 7.3.

Figure 7.3 Translating an Internet name

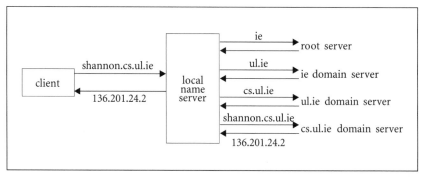

> The whole system is rather like phone books. We know the name of the person we want to phone, but we need a number. All of the phone numbers in the world are not listed in the one book. Each subscriber has a book of local numbers (the name server for the local domain). If they need a number not in the local book, they can apply to directory enquiries (higher level domain server). If directory enquiries do not have the number, they know where to get it (the root servers).

Caching

The system as it has just been described would work, but there would be an unacceptable number of queries travelling around the world. Instead, it relies heavily on caching. Every time a server sends a query for the address of another machine, it saves the name/address combination in memory. It always tries to satisfy a request from this cache before sending a query to another machine. When a server has been running for a while it will have all of the most frequently used addresses cached, and only rarely will it have to send queries over the network.

7.4 Operating systems

Two different types of underlying operating system have developed for use in distributed environments.

7.4.1 Network operating system

The most common use of a NOS is to attach file systems from a remote server on to a local machine, where they appear as part of the local directory structure. The user sees no difference between local and remote files. All of this is run on the server side by a network operating system, which is really just a general-purpose operating system with enhancements. It only transfers those portions of a file which are actually in use. If the file is modified, then the changes are written back to the server. There is a similarity between this and paging. Unix provides all of these services, as does Windows NT Server.

Such a NOS also allows other remote resources, such as a printer, to appear as if they were actually attached to the local machine.

7.4.2 Distributed operating system

A true distributed operating system must, at the very least, begin to blur the boundaries between machines.

Obviously it will be responsible for managing all local resources, such as the CPU and peripheral devices, including network interfaces. As well as this, it is responsible for advertising resources which are free and available, as well as exporting and importing processes to and from other machines. And it should do all of this transparently.

7.4.3 Hybrid systems

Fully distributed operating systems are not yet in widespread use. The current state of the art is to use specially adapted single-machine operating systems. These communicate among themselves, advertising resources which are free. So they are not fully transparent.

At present, the way forward is not clear. Several different alternatives have been proposed as the basis for the distributed systems of the future. We will consider two of these, but only time will tell exactly how the whole area will develop.

CORBA

The most important aspect of distributed design is the interface between the different components. Object orientation has been proposed as the best technique for defining such interfaces.

The Object Management Group has published a specification for a Common Object Request Broker Architecture. As its name implies, CORBA provides access to objects distributed across a system by matching up requests with objects. It is envisaged that CORBA would be used both for building distributed systems and for integrating existing and new applications.

In a distributed system, a server typically manages resources on behalf of clients. Like all object-oriented systems, CORBA encapsulates these resources in modules and makes them available only through interface procedures. This allows an application to be broken into components which can communicate with each other very easily, no matter where they are in the distributed system.

CORBA has been described as acting like a software bus. Just as hardware components all communicate with each other over the system bus, so software components communicate with each other through CORBA.

Within the Microsoft Windows environment, the Distributed Component Object Model (DCOM) performs a role similar to that of CORBA. Objects have DCOM interfaces which can be exported.

Distributed Computing Environment

The Open Software Foundation has developed DCE, which is an attempt to build a distributed computing environment on top of existing operating systems. It has been ported for example to Windows, OS/2, Tru64 Unix, and OpenVMS. So in theory you can take a number of existing machines, of different architectures, each running its own operating system, and just by putting the DCE software on top of these you have an instant distributed system, without disturbing any of the existing applications. In most cases this can be done at user level, without affecting the operating system itself.

In essence, DCE provides tools for building distributed applications, such as its own threads facility and services for running such distributed systems, including security and protection, a name service and a time server. The advantage is that all of these are integrated and do as much work as possible for the programmer.

7.5 Sockets

Any distributed system relies totally on the ability of different machines to communicate with one another. So we will now examine how such communication is implemented by the operating system on each machine. Then we will go on to consider how a distributed system could be built on top of the facilities provided by this layer.

7.5.1 The socket interface

The whole area of communication between machines is the province of computer networks. Despite the best efforts of the standards organisations, there are many different protocols or rules in use for communication between computers.

While there is no getting away from such differences, attempts have been made to provide one standard interface to all of these communication domains. One such mechanism is known as the socket interface. The socket facility is a set of system calls which allow processes to send and receive data across a network without having to worry about any of the underlying protocols. While it has not yet been standardized as part of POSIX, it is a *de facto* industry standard available on most systems, and is used in many network applications.

A top level view of the socket system is as follows. A process creates a socket, which begins life as just an anonymous data structure. Next it is uniquely identified within the whole system. Then this socket has to be connected with another socket in a different process. This can be done passively or actively. A process can wait to be contacted by another process or it can take the initiative. After this, data can be transferred across the connection. Finally a socket is closed and removed from the system. This sequence of operations, for both a server and a client, is outlined in Figure 7.4.

Figure 7.4 Communication using sockets

Server	Client
Create a socket	Create a socket
Bind an address	Bind an address
Listen for requests	
Accept a connection	Establish a connection
Receive	Send
Send	Receive

7.5.2 Creating a socket

While sockets can be created in several different flavours, there are two really important types. The first is connection-oriented, where it is assumed that a stream of data is going to flow between the sender and receiver. This is similar to the telephone service, where a connection is first set up, and after that you just talk. In the Internet domain these sockets are implemented by the Transmission Control Protocol (TCP).

The other type of socket is connectionless, or datagram, where the communication is going to be one or more individual messages. This is similar to the postal service, where each letter must be individually addressed. In the Internet domain these sockets are implemented by the User Datagram Protocol (UDP).

A socket is normally created as part of the I/O subsystem. It has a file descriptor and an entry in both the local and global file tables. It may or may not have a directory entry.

7.5.3 Binding an address

In the Internet domain, messages are sent over a network to a destination machine which is identified by an IP address. But each message also has an identifier for the protocol which should receive it, such as UDP or TCP. Then within the particular Internet protocol, a 16 bit number, called a port number, is used to identify the specific socket. So a connection between two sockets is fully specified by source IP address, source port, protocol in use, destination port and destination IP address.

Assigning a port number to a socket is known as binding.

7.5.4 Connecting sockets

A stream socket can wait passively to be contacted or it can actively connect to another socket.

Accepting connections
Let us first look at the passive situation. This is typical with servers, where they set themselves up, and wait for clients to contact them. First of all the process which created the socket specifies a particular port number to be associated with it. This port number is usually well known in network circles. Then it blocks, listening for requests to that port. When a request for connection does come in, a new socket is created to handle it, and the original one continues to listen at the well-known port number for further requests.

Setting up a connection
A client can ask the system to connect it to a remote socket. For this, it must be able to identify the machine (e.g. IP address), the protocol (e.g. TCP) and the port number of the socket listening at the other end. Once a connection has been established, data can then be transferred across it.

7.6 Remote procedure call

The socket mechanism provides a way of transmitting data between processes on different machines. It can be used to implement a client/ server system. A request is sent, and then the requesting process waits until the result arrives. This looks very much like the traditional I/O system to a user. It was one logical way to develop distributed systems, building on what programmers were used to.

But programmers are probably even more familiar with function calls. Such a function call diverts control to an out-of-line function, possibly passing parameters to it as well. When the function finishes, control returns to the main program and a result value is also made available in the main program. So another possible way to develop distributed systems is to implement a mechanism which would allow programs to call functions on other machines. In this way, all the details of how the network operates (even its existence) can be hidden from the application program.

7.6.1 Overview

The remote machine has a module containing one or more procedures. This gives the mechanism its name – remote procedure call, or RPC. We try to make it look like a normal function call as far as possible – input and output parameters, and a return value. This is achieved by the client having a dummy procedure in a library on its own machine, known as a stub. The client calls this in the usual way, just like any other local procedure. As far as the client knows, this is the procedure which is doing the work. But it is not. All it does is to format the parameters into a message, add some identification of the procedure it wants executed on the remote machine, and send the message off to that machine using an interface such as a socket. The client stub then blocks, waiting for a reply.

When the message arrives at the remote machine, the RPC server process there unpacks the message, and identifies which procedure is being requested. It then calls that procedure in the normal way and the procedure returns as normal, passing back a return value to the RPC server process. This in turn packages the result as a message, and sends it to the communication layer for transmission back to the waiting stub on the requesting machine. This stub is then woken up, unpacks the message and passes back the result to the client process in the normal way. Figure 7.5 illustrates the flow of control in this case.

7.6.2 Generating stubs

All of this could be done by hand, in a conventional programming language, but it would be very prone to error. The order and type of the parameters must be the same in all four modules that deal with them. If all four are coded independently, there is certainly room for inconsistencies to creep in, particularly over time, as changes are made in one place but not in all.

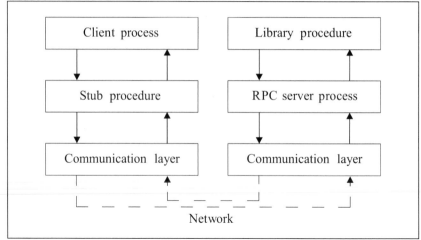

Figure 7.5 Call/return with RPC

Network

The ideal is to automate as much of this as possible. The programmer only writes the client program and the server procedure. Tools have been developed which generate C code to implement RPC. They are supplied with the characteristics of remote procedures that are visible to clients, such as the name of the procedure and the number and types of the parameters. From this specification they generate a server stub and a client stub, which make the network calls. These are then compiled and linked in with the code written by the programmer.

7.7 Distributed mutual exclusion

Now that we have developed interfaces for communication between machines, such as sockets and RPC, we can go on to consider how these can be used to implement distributed versions of the services that a standalone operating system provides for its local processes.

We have looked at the problems connected with concurrent systems on a single machine in some detail. When studying mutual exclusion on standalone machines, we based our solutions on the idea of critical sections within programs. Then, once we had guaranteed that at most one process could be executing a critical section at any time, we could guarantee mutual exclusion. Mechanisms such as semaphores were introduced to control this. Now we turn to the extra complications introduced when concurrent processes are running on different machines.

The concept of critical sections will extend to cover mutual exclusion in distributed systems. But mechanisms such as semaphores are difficult to distribute. They rely on shared variables, which by definition exist in one place. It is difficult to guarantee indivisible uninterruptible access to them over a network.

So other algorithms have been developed to control mutual exclusion in distributed systems. These fall into two classes.

7.7.1   Centralized algorithm

With this arrangement, there is one dedicated coordinator process somewhere in the system. Such a process could control one critical section or many. When a process wishes to enter its critical section, it asks permission from this coordinator, waits until it gets it, enters the critical section, and then informs the coordinator when it leaves its critical section. The coordinator must ensure that only one process has permission to be in its critical section at any time.

Such a system will work if there are no failures or lost messages. One problem with it, as with all centralized algorithms, is that it introduces a communications bottleneck. Also the whole system will deadlock if a process crashes while in its critical section. But the main problem with any centralized algorithm is that the coordinator process may crash. Such systems are usually built so that any process can act as coordinator, but only one does so at a time. So when the current coordinator crashes, it is necessary to ensure that another one takes over – but only one other.

There must be some way of recognising that the coordinator is no longer functioning. This can usually be detected by failure to receive an acknowledgement after a timeout period. The process which detects the lack of a coordinator identifies a successor from among all of the others based on the combination of process id and IP address, which we assume is globally unique. Generally, the process with the highest id is selected as coordinator. Two processes can discover a dead coordinator at the same time, but both will identify the one new coordinator.

7.7.2   A distributed algorithm

Because of the drawbacks associated with centralized algorithms, fully distributed algorithms have been developed. With these, each process takes its share of the responsibility for arranging mutual exclusion on a critical section. Such an algorithm assumes that all processes know each other.

When a process wants to enter its critical section, it multicasts a request to all of the others. A process will only reply to this request if it is not in, or wanting to go into, its critical section. The requesting process waits until it has got permission from all of the others, then enters its critical section.

One of the drawbacks of this algorithm is the large number of messages it requires. Another problem is the need to know all the processes involved. But it is suitable for small, stable sets of cooperating processes.

7.8 Deadlock in distributed systems

Deadlock is a problem even in standalone systems. When we move to a system of cooperating machines the situation becomes even more complicated, as do the solutions.

Deadlock prevention is not used in distributed environments, as it has been found to be unacceptably restrictive even in standalone systems.

Nor is deadlock avoidance used in distributed systems. Remember, avoidance algorithms need advance knowledge of all the resources required by processes. This is difficult, if not impossible, to know even in a standalone system, and is really only relevant to batch systems. Once we move into distributed computing, it is not feasible to talk about advance knowledge of all resource usage.

That leaves us with deadlock detection and recovery. Each individual machine maintains its own local resource allocation graph, typically in a reduced form which only records dependencies between processes, known as a wait-for graph. Then the problem is to check for cycles in the union of all of these graphs. When such a cycle exists, one process is chosen and aborted. Of course that presupposes that we know how to maintain and check a wait-for graph for a whole distributed system.

The algorithm to implement this can be centralized or distributed.

7.8.1   Centralized algorithm

Each machine maintains a graph for its own resources, and could even implement local detection and recovery. Then there is a coordinator process which maintains the union of these graphs.

A process could send a message to the coordinator each time a local graph is changed. Or it could send messages about the state of the local graph periodically. Or the coordinator could ask for information at fixed intervals.

The coordinator examines the distributed graph periodically. There could be a cycle in this distributed graph which is not in any local one, so indicating a distributed deadlock.

For example, the resource allocator on machine A sees the graph on the left of Figure 7.6. The resource allocator on machine B sees the graph in the centre of Figure 7.6. Neither of these has a cycle, so there does not appear to be any deadlock. But the coordinator sees the union of the two graphs, as shown on the right of Figure 7.6. Clearly there is a system-wide cycle, and these four processes are deadlocked.

Figure 7.6 Local and global wait-for graphs

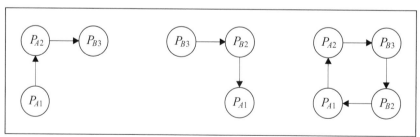

7.8.2   Distributed algorithm

Every time a transaction has to wait for a resource, it sends a message to the process holding it. This message contains the id of the blocked process. If the recipient is waiting on something, it updates the message with its own id and forwards it to the process holding that resource. If the message ever comes back to the original sender, then there is a cycle.

This scheme is attractive, but sending a message when you are blocked is not exactly trivial.

7.8.3 Recovery

Discovering a cycle in a distributed system is one thing. But then there is the question of how to break a cycle when one is discovered. There are two options available: either kill one or more processes or preempt some resources from one or more processes.

One possibility is for the blocked process to terminate itself. But this could be overkill if more than one process discovers the cycle at about the same time. With the distributed algorithm, each blocked process could add its id number to the message instead of replacing it. This way the ids of all processes involved in the cycle would be known to all of the others. The highest or lowest could then choose itself as victim.

7.9 Distributed shared memory

We have seen how shared memory is implemented for processes running on the same machine. And we have seen how this is the basic mechanism underpinning all interprocess communication on standalone machines. Data is passed between cooperating processes through shared buffers. Synchronisation and mutual exclusion are implemented using semaphores, which are basically shared variables.

Effort is now being directed towards allowing memory to be shared by processes on different machines. This would allow a shared memory programming model to be used by cooperating processes in a distributed system. With such a scheme, a standalone system could be distributed with minimum effort.

7.9.1 Implementation

To a programmer, there should be no difference between distributed shared memory and shared memory on a standalone machine. Each process has its own virtual address space. Some of the physical memory backing this address space is also mapped into the address space of other processes. Whether these processes are on the same machine or on remote machines should not really be relevant to a programmer.

On a standalone machine there is no question about where the shared memory will be physically located – it will have to be somewhere in the physical memory of that machine. But with a distributed system, it could physically exist on any of the machines.

The simplest way to implement distributed shared memory is to have one server machine which manages the shared memory on behalf of client processes on remote machines. These communicate with the server by means of RPC.

The initial mapping of a range of such distributed shared memory into the address space of a process can be handled in a manner very similar to POSIX shared memory. An initial RPC identifies the block of shared memory which is being requested. The server checks permissions and access mode etc., and then returns a handle. This is a unique identifier which is used to identify and authenticate all further accesses to that block of distributed shared memory.

The server exports two further procedures, one for reading, and one for writing. Finally there is a procedure which lets the server know that the client has no further use for this block of shared memory.

7.9.2 Local run-time support

While easy to understand, the foregoing scheme is very inefficient and can be improved on in a number of ways. So far, the local memory manager is not involved at all – the client process has to make an RPC for every read and write. Ideally, distributed shared memory should be transparent to a process. Assignment to variables in distributed shared memory should be identical to assignment to variables in local memory – the memory manager should take care of all of the necessary overhead.

This can be accomplished by a slight extension to the local memory manager and to the mmap() system service so that it can map this shared memory into the address map of the process, possibly setting it up as a segment in its own right. Then it returns a pointer to this segment. From here on the process accesses the distributed shared memory using standard local pointers.

The first time a program references an address which is not local a remote page fault occurs, and the distributed shared memory run-time fetches the appropriate page. To a user, this looks exactly like the traditional system. The main difference is that the backing store is a remote server, not a local disk.

7.10 Distributed file systems

We have already studied file systems in a previous chapter. A first step up from such a standalone system is the ability to copy files between different machines, such as is provided by the file transfer protocol, ftp. This makes a second copy of the file on the local machine. A distributed file system is much more than that. There is only one copy of the file, but it appears as if it exists on any of the machines in the system. Such a file system can be part of a distributed operating system, but this is not necessary. A distributed file system should look like a conventional file system, including its performance.

7.10.1 Client/server systems

The simplest way to implement a distributed file system is to have the files on one machine (the server) and the user on another machine (the client). In a realistic system there will be many clients, and possibly more than one server. Servers can run on dedicated machines, or a machine can be both server and client.

Typically, a user would make normal system calls which the client software translates to RPC calls to the server.

A server can track each file being accessed by each client. It can implement locks and perform read-ahead for sequential reads, just like a standalone file system. All of this implies that it must maintain information about every file that each client has opened, and that this information must be maintained until the file is closed. Because of this, it is known as a stateful server. Such a server can be in difficulties after a crash, when all of this information is lost. It will not know about which files any particular client has open.

Another possibility is that it can simply provide blocks as requested. In this case the server does not keep track of which clients are accessing which files. Such a stateless server is slower, but it is more robust, in that it simplifies the recovery procedures after a server crashes and reboots. A client must provide a stateless server with a filename and offset at each request. No open or close requests are sent to the server.

7.10.2 Naming schemes

One basic problem for any distributed file system is to provide a namespace that uniquely identifies each file in the system. File systems have traditionally used directories for this, organized in some form of tree or graph structure.

At one end of the scale, such a distributed system could be implemented by integrating all files and directories into a single global namespace spanning all machines in the system. The complexity of administering such a namespace, particularly if the file system is distributed over many machines, outweighs any benefits it may bring.

At the other end of the scale, a two-part naming scheme, such as host:localname, would be relatively easy to implement but would not be location transparent. A user would have to know exactly where each file was in the system.

A middle of the road approach is normally acceptable. Remote file systems are attached to local systems and appear seamlessly as just another part of the local system. A user should not be able to tell the difference between a local directory and a remote one. Obviously both the exporting and the importing machine would need extra software.

Figure 7.7 shows two simple file systems, one on a local machine and the other on a remote machine. Figure 7.8 shows the situation on the local machine after it has attached the contents of the remote directory 'projects' to its directory 'programs'. Note that both of these files still exist on the remote machine; they only appear as if they were attached to the

Figure 7.7 Situation before attaching remote files

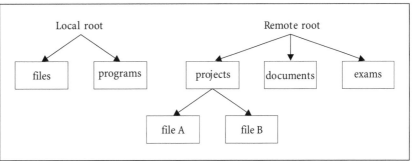

local 'programs' directory. Note also that the local machine must know where they are in order to attach them, but after that all references to these files are transparent. Finally, the original contents of the 'programs' directory on the local machine are no longer visible. They are still there, but cannot be accessed again until the remote directory has been detached.

Figure 7.8 Local file system after attaching remote files

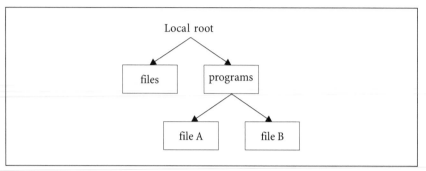

7.10.3 Reading and writing

The set of requests which the client can make on the server are normally very similar to the standard POSIX system services for files, but are implemented as synchronous remote procedure calls. This means that the client blocks until the server replies.

On a client machine, the system calls and all of the high-level processing are identical for local and remote files. The local operating system determines whether a file is local or remote at open(). If it is a local file, then it is handled by its own particular file system code. If the file is a remote one, then the operations field in its global file table entry points to functions supplied by the distributed file system (DFS). Figure 7.9 illustrates how the RPC mechanism is integrated with the virtual file system.

7.10.4 Caching

A server will normally cache directories or blocks of a file to save on disk accesses. This is just normal file system buffering, and presents no extra problems.

A client will also cache file blocks to avoid the delays associated with using a network and to reduce the volume of traffic on the network, as well as the load on the server.

There is a problem keeping cached copies of a shared file consistent with the original and with each other. There are a number of approaches to this.

▶ **Write-through** Any write to cached data is also written to the server. Write-through is very reliable, but it implies heavy overheads. It really uses the cache only for reading.

▶ **Delayed-write** A write to cached data is not passed on to the server immediately, but at fixed intervals.

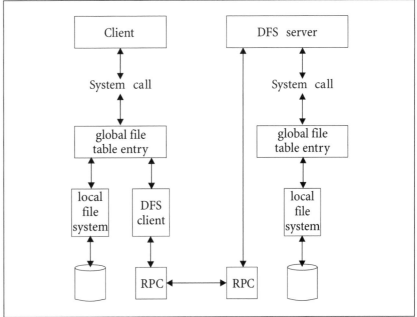

Figure 7.9 Handling local and remote file systems

▶ **Write-on-close** Writes are only visible to other processes when a file is closed. In this case, if two processes are writing then the last one to close overwrites anything written by the other one.

7.10.5 Replication

Multiple copies of the same file may be kept on different servers to increase reliability and to distribute the workload over the system. This is not just caching, but permanently replicating resources in their entirety.

Replication should be transparent to the user, implemented by the system. Each replica manager retains a physical copy of some or all files. These replica managers can periodically swap updates.

Replication of read only files is trivial, but it does ensure availability when one of the servers is down. If requests are processed in parallel by all of the replica servers, then it is even fault-tolerant. But once writable files are replicated there are questions of consistency if some are updated and others not.

7.10.6 Sun Network File System

One of the most commonly used file systems is NFS. It was originally de-signed as part of SunOS, the operating system for Sun workstations. The definitions of its protocols are in the public domain, which led to its wide-spread adoption so that it has become a *de facto* standard. It has been im-plemented on top of a range of different hardware and operating systems.

NFS maintains only one copy of a file, and the most recent update is the version visible to the system. Any replication or caching is extra, not part of NFS. As several clients can import the same directory, sharing is implicit in the system. This sharing is controlled by the access permission mechanism on the server.

> Implementations of distributed file systems will be required to scale well to the very large systems of the future, possibly even worldwide systems. This rules out any mechanisms which rely on centralisation. Broadcasting, or sending a message to all machines on the network, is another mechanism which does not scale well to larger systems. So there will be more emphasis placed on fully distributed algorithms.

CHAPTER SUMMARY

▶ A distributed system is a collection of networked computers which cooperate to distribute computation among themselves.

▶ There are a number of reasons leading to the development of distributed systems. There are economic reasons, as a network of small machines is cheaper than the equivalent large machine. Also, they can offer greater reliability. The ability to share resources is another factor, as well as their ability to grow little by little.

▶ We prefer to identify machines and resources by human-readable names. At the systems level this is more conveniently done by numeric identifiers. A name server maps between the two.

DNS is the name server used for the Internet. It is a distributed database which makes heavy use of caching.

▶ Network operating systems provide some distributed applications, such as remote directory and printer sharing. A true distributed operating system must go further than this, and at least begin to blur the boundaries between machines.

CORBA provides access to distributed objects. It can be used both for building new systems and for distributing legacy systems. The interface definition is at the heart of the CORBA system.

OSF DCE is a similar proposal which also runs on top of existing operating systems. It provides tools for building distributed applications as well as run-time services to support them.

▶ Interprocess communication between different machines is an essential prerequisite for any distributed system. The socket facility allows processes to send and receive data across a network without having to worry about any of the underlying mechanisms.

After a socket is created, it can then be assigned a unique system-wide id number. A user may passively accept connections or may actually take the initiative and establish a link with a remote socket which is listening. After that, data can be passed between the two ends.

▶ Remote procedure call is a mechanism which allows programs to call functions on remote machines in a transparent manner. The caller has a stub procedure to marshal the arguments into a message and send it to the server. The server has a stub which unmarshals the arguments and calls the actual worker procedure.

Some of the work involved in writing RPC programs can be automated.

▶ The algorithms which have been developed to control mutual exclusion in distributed systems fall into two classes. Some are centralized, with one controller which handles all requests. If this controller crashes, a new one has to be elected.

Another possibility is to control mutual exclusion using a fully distributed algorithm. For example, a process could request permission from all of the others before entering its critical section.

▶ Deadlock prevention and avoidance are not used in distributed systems. Detection and recovery can be implemented with either a centralized or a distributed algorithm.

▶ A server manages distributed shared memory for a group of clients. These send requests to the server using RPC. On a local machine, the onus could be put on the memory manager to mask any difference between local and remote memory.

▶ A distributed file system allows a file on one machine to appear as if it actually existed on another machine. The system consists of a file server and a client. A user makes normal system calls, which are translated to RPC calls to a server. Such a distributed file system can provide stateful or stateless service.

It must be possible to identify each file in the system in a way that is location-independent. A typical solution is to allow remote directories to be mounted as part of a local directory tree.

Caching of files on the client is used to reduce network traffic, and improve performance. The major drawback with it is the problem of cache consistency.

Multiple copies of the same file may be kept on different servers to increase reliability and to distribute the workload over the system. With writable files, such replication introduces problems of transparency and consistency.

The Sun Network File System is a commonly used distributed file system.

FURTHER READING

A general introduction to distributed systems and the design issues involved can be found in Silberschatz and Galvin Sections 15.1, 15.2 and 16.5; Tanenbaum (1992) Chapter 9; Tanenbaum (1995) Chapter 1. Client/server architecture is dealt with in Stallings Section 12.3; Tanenbaum (1992) Section 10.2; Tanenbaum (1995) Section 2.3. Tanenbaum deals with system models in (1992) Section 12.2 and (1995) Section 4.2; and processor allocation in (1992) Section 12.3 and (1995) Section 4.3. Stallings Section 13.1 covers process migration. Silberschatz and Galvin deal with network operating systems in Section 16.1 and distributed operating systems in Section 16.2. Tanenbaum (1995) introduces DCE in Chapter 10.

An introduction to communication in distributed systems is given in Stallings Section 12.1. Sockets are introduced by Silberschatz and Galvin Section 21.9.1. Socket programming is covered by Robbins and Robbins Section 12.4; Gray Chapter 10; Rago Chapter 7.

For an overview of RPC see Silberschatz and Galvin Section 16.3.1; Nutt Section 17.3; Stallings Section 12.5; Tanenbaum (1992) Section 10.3; Tanenbaum (1995) Section 2.4. RPC programming is covered by Robbins and Robbins Chapter 14; Gray Chapter 9; Rago Chapter 8.

Silberschatz and Galvin deal with distributed services in Chapter 18, as does Tanenbaum (1995) in Chapter 3 and Tanenbaum (1992) in Chapter 11. Stallings deals specifically with distributed deadlocks in Section 13.4. For further reading on distributed shared memory, see Tanenbaum (1995) Chapter 6 or Nutt Section 17.4. For a general introduction to distributed file systems, see Silberschatz and Galvin Chapter 17; Nutt Chapter 16; Tanenbaum (1992) Chapter 13; Tanenbaum (1995) Chapter 5. Material specific to NFS can be found in Silberschatz and Galvin Section 17.6.2.

SELF-TEST QUESTIONS

1   Outline five features which are specific to distributed systems and are influencing the pace of their development.

2   Explain the role of a nameserver in a distributed system.

3   Explain how the Internet DNS translates a name to an address.

4   Distinguish between a network operating system and a fully distributed operating system.

5   Outline the approach to building distributed systems taken by CORBA and by DCE.

6   Outline the steps involved in setting up communication using a stream socket, both on the server side and on the client side.

7   Give an overview of the RPC mechanism.

8   Explain both the centralized and distributed approach to mutual exclusion in a distributed system.

9   Explain both the centralized and distributed approaches to deadlock in a distributed system.

10 Describe how distributed shared memory could be implemented.

11 Explain the difference between stateful and stateless distributed file systems.

12 Explain how a remote file system can be integrated into the directory structure of a local machine.

13 Outline some different approaches to keeping cached copies of shared files consistent with the original and with each other.

DISCUSSION QUESTIONS

1 A distributed system can be built to be so reliable and fault-tolerant that a user need not even be aware that a fault has occurred. Is this a good thing?

2 Investigate the `nslookup` program and use it to obtain information about different subdomains of the Internet.

3 When you present a name to your browser or mailer, how does it find out the address of the machine it has to communicate with? Work out all of the steps involved.

4 Which communication protocols are in use on the machine you use?

5 The socket facility can be built on top of many different communication domains. Why does this not allow a machine using DECNET to communicate with a machine using AppleTalk? What extra arrangements would have to be made to allow this?

6 Consult the manual page for `socket()` (or a textbook) to find out more about the differences between stream and datagram sockets, as well as any other types which might be available.

7 The same system service, `bind()`, is used to associate an address with a socket, no matter which address domain is in use. How can one function be so universal?

8 When a request comes in to a socket awaiting connections, a new socket is created to handle it and the original socket continues to listen for further requests. What address does the new socket have, how does it get it, and how does the requesting socket get to know it?

9 For a conventional function call (e.g. a user-defined function or a client stub), how are the parameters actually passed? How is the return value passed back?

10 An RPC server could have one general-purpose module which receives all requests and then passes them on to the appropriate local procedure. Or it may have a separate stub for each procedure. What are the advantages and disadvantages of each method?

11 Investigate some algorithms for electing a new coordinator when a centralized algorithm is used for mutual exclusion.

12. What happens if a centralized coordinator crashes, is replaced, and then starts up again, acting as if it were still the coordinator?

13 Is the distributed algorithm for mutual exclusion fair?

14 Develop a distributed algorithm for mutual exclusion based on token passing.

15 Discuss how each of the four necessary conditions for deadlock might be negated in a distributed system.

16 Outline the requirements of a distributed shared memory system in which different parts of the memory are owned by different machines.

17 Could the local run-time support for distributed shared memory be extended so that a program could actually declare a distributed shared variable and refer to it by name?

18 If two clients have the same file cached using write-through caching, can they interfere with each other? What solutions are available for this problem?

19 Suggest a protocol which replica managers could use among themselves to keep their copies of a file consistent.

20 With NFS, could a client mount the same remote directory at two different points in its own directory tree?

Fault tolerance and security

CHAPTER OVERVIEW

This final chapter introduces you to how operating systems deal with threats to their correct functioning, including fault handling and security issues, in both standalone and distributed systems.

Having read this chapter, you should understand:

▶ the issues involved in handling faults in computer systems

▶ the mechanisms used to implement security policies on standalone systems

▶ the extra implications of security in distributed systems, including authentication and cryptography

8.1 Fault tolerance

How well a system can deal with faults is the area of fault tolerance.

8.1.1 Types of fault

A fault is a malfunction, the cause of an error. It can be a hardware or a software fault. It can be transient, intermittent, or permanent.

A transient fault occurs once only. It is usually a hardware fault, such as a random cosmic ray flipping a bit in memory. There is not much that can be done about identifying the fault and repairing it, as it does not occur again. The emphasis is on detecting it and recovering from it.

An intermittent fault occurs again and again, at unpredictable intervals. It is the most difficult type of fault to diagnose, as you never know when it will occur again. It can be a failing hardware component or a bug in software.

A permanent fault is just that – something is broken and must be replaced. This can be a hardware component or a piece of code which is not doing what it is supposed to do.

8.1.2 Detecting faults

The first requirement for a fault-tolerant system is that it be able to detect a fault. This should be done as soon as possible, as the longer it goes undetected the more errors will be caused, reducing the chance of identifying the underlying fault.

The general approach to this is to use redundancy. Data faults can be detected by using information redundancy, such as check-bits or checksums. They can indicate that a data item has been corrupted. A step up from this is to use error-correcting codes. There is a greater overhead involved here, but they make it possible to recreate the correct value.

Another possibility is to use time redundancy by repeating the operation. For example, two different copies of a file can be read and compared. If they do not match exactly, we know that an error has occurred. This more than doubles the time involved. Sometimes it is possible to use physical redundancy by installing extra equipment, e.g. duplicate processing on two different CPUs.

8.1.3 Recovering from faults

When a fault-tolerant system detects a fault, it either fails gracefully or masks it. Graceful failure means that it informs the user, notifies any other processes it is communicating with, closes all I/O streams it has open, returns memory, and stops the process. Masking a fault would include retrying an operation on a different CPU, attempting to contact a different server on a network, using a different software routine, or using an alternative source for data.

At the very least, faults should be confined to the process in which they occur. They must not spread to other processes or to the operating system itself.

8.1.4 Faults in file systems

The following are some common faults which are specific to file systems.

▶ Bad read. One or more sectors of a disk cannot be read. At best, the user loses part of a file. At worst, a whole directory, an index block or a bitmap can be lost.

▶ Bad write. Information is written to the wrong sector. Chains of pointers can be corrupted. One file can be linked into another or, even worse, into the free list, resulting in chaos.

▶ When a system uses a disk buffer cache, a power failure can leave the disk in an inconsistent state.

▶ Viruses can cause corruption or even total loss of data.

▶ There are always faults attributable to humans, whether intentional or not.

Precautions
In designing safeguards against these faults, the following factors have to be balanced.

▶ What is the mean time between failure (MTBF) for the hardware? In other words, what are the odds against the system crashing?

> ▷ What is the operational cost of making backup copies? If it only requires a click on an icon or can be done automatically, then why not do it? But in some systems it may mean shutting the computer down.

> ▷ What is the cost of loss of information? The loss of the latest version of a student program is very different from the loss of banking information.

One hundred per cent protection requires that everything be recorded in duplicate or triplicate. This involves two or three similar drives, all writing in unison. Reads are also duplicated and compared.

Another security feature is to read after every write to check that the data has been properly written. This involves a heavy time overhead.

Backups and recovery
Generally some degree of loss can be tolerated, and the policy adopted is regular backups.

One approach to this is to do a total backup at fixed intervals. The entire file system is copied to tape or to another disk. Recovery from a crash is easy when using a total backup. The disk is reformatted or replaced, and the backup tape is copied to the disk. We then have a copy of the file system as it was a day, a week or a month ago.

8.1.5   Faults in distributed systems

Distributed systems involve a number of machines and a communications infrastructure which can be spread over quite a wide area. Hence by their nature such systems are more prone to faults than standalone machines. But these same characteristics can be used to ensure that the system as a whole can survive faults. With a multiplicity of machines, a distributed system can be designed so that faulty or non-functioning elements of the system, whether processors, disk storage or communications, can be replaced by other fully functioning elements.

8.2   Security

There may also be deliberate attempts to cause the system to malfunction, and this is the area of security.

Threats to security come at different levels. Leakage happens when confidential information is accidentally made available to an unauthorized agent. Stealing is when such an agent takes positive action to access the information. Tampering is when data in the system is changed in such a way that it still appears to be valid. Vandalism is when data is changed so as to be meaningless.

Once there is more than one user, or even more than one process, on a machine, it becomes necessary to provide some security protection.

8.2.1   Security policy

A security policy is a statement of the rules and practices that regulate how a computer system manages, protects and distributes sensitive information. The security policy decides whether a given subject (user, process etc.) can be permitted to gain access to a specific object (resource, data, file etc.). A computer system should have sufficient hardware and software to enforce such a security policy.

Each user has a set of privileges which give rights to access certain objects through operating system functions. These privileges are acquired when a user logs on to the system, and are normally inherited by each new process that the user creates.

8.2.2 Protection mechanisms

Protection can be implemented in many different ways, from an all-or-nothing level down to a very fine granularity. Generally there is a trade-off between the granularity of the protection and the overhead of implementing it.

Physical exclusion
If the system can only be accessed from specific terminals in a designated area, then traditional security methods such as locks or identity checks can be used to control access to those terminals. This level of protection is normally only used in the highest security sites.

Exclusion of unauthorized users
The traditional approach to this is to issue each user with an account name and a password. The problems with passwords are well known. Many systems will not allow a user to set a password which is easily cracked. It is common practice that only encrypted versions of passwords are stored, and the encryption algorithm cannot be reversed.

Distinguishing between users
We do not, however, want even authorized users to have access to everything. So we must make some further distinctions *after* access. The system maintains a list of the privileges granted to each user and checks every request for resources against this.

This is certainly an improvement, but it still has the weakness that access rights remain unchanged during the lifetime of a process. A process may need access to a particular resource just once, for example at initialisation. But it retains that right, even though it is unneeded. This is a potential security hole.

Access for current activity only
The most fine-grained protection is based on the idea of need-to-know, or access rights for the current activity only.

For example, consider two processes performing two-way communication through a shared buffer. Access privileges for the buffer segment should be dependent on whether a process is currently engaged in reading or writing. So we need mechanisms for granting and revoking privileges while a process is running.

8.2.3   Access matrix

The most general way of tracking who can access what, and how, in a system is to use an access matrix.

The rows of the matrix represent processes, also known as subjects or domains. This is the 'who' part. The columns represent the resources, or objects. This is the 'what'. The entries in the array represent the 'how' part.

Figure 8.1 shows an example of a simple access matrix.

Figure 8.1 Example access matrix

	File1	File2	File3	CDdrive	Printer
Domain1	Read		Read		
Domain2				Read	Print
Domain3		Read	Execute		
Domain4	Read/Write		Read/Write		

The information in the access matrix should not be accessible to user-level processes. It itself is highly protected by the operating system.

An access matrix for even a small system can grow quite large. Most of the entries will be empty. Such a sparse matrix is very wasteful of space. So they are rarely implemented as actual matrices. Other methods are used, purely to pack the relevant data in more concisely. We will now consider some of these.

Global table
Each entry in such a table is a set of ordered triples <Domain, Object, RightsSet>. For example, the information from the first row of Figure 8.1 would be encapsulated as <Domain1, File1, Read>, <Domain1, File3, Read>.

If the triple corresponding to a particular operation exists, then that operation is valid. Otherwise it is invalid.

Even though it does not take up as much space as a full access matrix, such a table can be quite large. Also, if a particular object can be accessed by every subject, then it must have a separate entry corresponding to each domain. This tends to inflate the size of the table.

Capability lists
One way of slicing the access matrix is to have a separate list for each domain. This would consist of the couples <Object, RightsSet>. As such a list specifies what a subject operating in that domain can do, not surprisingly it is known as a capability list. The capability list for Domain1 in Figure 8.1 would be <File1, Read>, <File3, Read>.

Access control lists
Another way of compacting an access matrix is to store each column in the matrix as a separate list of ordered pairs <Domain, RightsSet>. With this scheme, each object has its own access control list. For example, the

access list for File1 in Figure 8.1 would be <Domain1, Read>, <Domain4, Read/Write>.

If there are any default access rights, these could be put at the head of the list, e.g. <AllDomains, RightsSet>. So the defaults would be checked first before going on to scan the remainder of the list.

8.3 Security in distributed systems

Security in a distributed system involves two further aspects: authentication of the different machines and users in the system and the protection of messages passing between them.

8.3.1 Authentication

This involves the set of techniques whereby a server can identify a remote user or a client can verify that it is dealing with a legitimate server.

Servers themselves are always in danger of being infiltrated. The best known method is still password cracking. Viruses are another way to get control of a server. A virus (in this context) is a program which can modify another program, such as the part of the operating system implementing the security policy.

One-way authentication
The classic mechanism for a user to authenticate itself to a server has been passwords. An improvement for standalone machines would be non-forgeable identifiers, such as fingerprints or voice patterns. These are difficult to transmit over a network, and so are of less value in a distributed system.

Two-way authentication
It is not sufficient for a machine to authenticate a user; the user must also be able to authenticate the machine. It is important to know that it is the legitimate server and not a fake. A common method is to have one trusted authentication server in the system. Each machine can agree a password with this server.

For example, a user wishing to log on to a file server would send its request through the authentication server. This can verify the user and authenticate the request to the file server. It can also verify the file server and assure the user that it is dealing with the authorized server.

8.3.2 Cryptography

Data passing over communications lines is particularly vulnerable to attack. Eavesdropping on the line is the simplest way of stealing data. Masquerading as a legitimate source of messages is another way of obtaining unauthorized information. Or valid messages can be intercepted and tampered with, causing servers to perform unauthorized actions. Another technique is to store copies of messages, and replay them at a later time.

> For example, authorisation to an ATM to issue money could be replayed later in the hope of getting the machine to issue the money again.

The whole aim of cryptography is to conceal private information from unauthorized eyes. The sender uses a rule to transform the data into an unintelligible encrypted form; the recipient uses an inverse rule. However, if an intruder discovers the rule, then all secrecy is lost.

An improvement on a rule is a function with a key as a parameter. This relies on the secure distribution and storage of keys. Cryptography using keys also involves authentication, as possession of the appropriate encryption or decryption key can be used to authenticate the sender or receiver. Modern systems are moving towards authentication servers which both authenticate users and issue keys. Of course this is putting all of the eggs in one basket. If an intruder gains access to this server, all security is broken. It is now accepted that such security systems need to be rigidly designed using formal methods.

In general, encryption schemes can use either secret or public keys.

Secret key encryption

The key is issued in two forms. One is used to encrypt messages. Another, which can be sent securely to the recipient, is used to decrypt them. But secure distribution of keys is a problem.

One possibility is to use an authentication server to distribute them. Such a server maintains a table of <name, secret key> pairs, which is used to authenticate clients.

Suppose, for example, a client A wishes to communicate secretly with B. It first authenticates itself to the server by sending a message encrypted with its secret key. This message asks for a key to communicate with its destination B. This is the first of the sequence of messages illustrated in Figure 8.2.

The server uses A's secret key to decrypt this message, so proving that it must have come from A. It then generates a one-off key for this communication between A and B, and sends this key, as well as a copy of this key encrypted with B's secret key, back to A. This whole message is encrypted with A's secret key, so A can decrypt it. This is the second message in Figure 8.2.

A then sends the encrypted version of the one-off key to B. As the server originally encrypted this with B's secret key, B is able to decrypt it and extract the one-off key. A never learns B's secret key.

Then A encrypts its message using the one-off key, and sends this encrypted message to B. B uses the one-off key to decrypt it, thus proving that it must have come from A.

Public key encryption

Each recipient has two keys, such that either can be used to decrypt a message encrypted with the other. One, the private key, is kept very secret. The other, the public key, is freely available, e.g. on the Web. Anyone can encrypt a message with the public key, but only the recipient can decrypt it, using the private key.

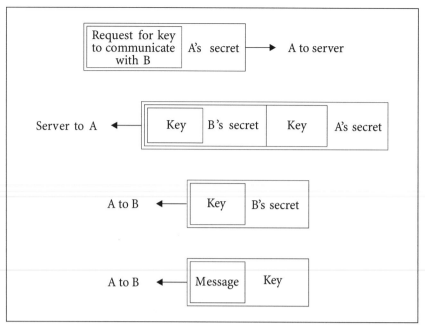

Figure 8.2 Sequence of messages
with secret keys

8.3.3 Digital signatures

With the growth in the number of computer documents, we need to be able to authenticate such documents. Again, either public or secret keys can be used for this.

Public keys
The document is encrypted with the private key. Anyone can decrypt it using the public key, but only the originator could have encrypted it. So its authenticity is guaranteed.

Secret keys
This requires the use of an authentication server. The source process sends the message, encrypted with its secret key, to this server, which verifies the sender. The server then adds a certificate of authenticity, and encrypts the message with the secret key of the destination process. The receiver has the assurance of the server it trusts that the message is authentic. Figure 8.3 shows the sequence of operations in this case.

CHAPTER SUMMARY

▷ Computer systems are particularly prone to faults. The first step is to detect them. Then a system can try to mask them in some way, such as reconfiguring the system to work around the faulty element.
  Users must have confidence that their files will be there when required. Disks do fail, so operating systems have procedures built into them to recover from such failures. The simplest method is frequent backups.

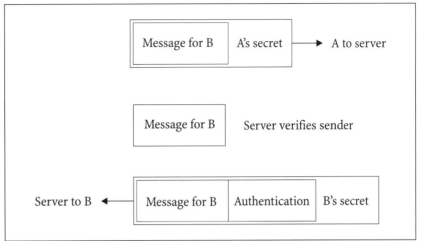

Figure 8.3 Digital signature with secret key

Distributed systems are more prone to faults, but faulty components can easily be masked by functioning ones.

▶ Threats to security do not just come from malicious outsiders, but can also result from faults within the system itself.

Modern computer systems are expected to have a formal description of just how secure they are.

Protection mechanisms can range from physical exclusion, through exclusion of unauthorized users, then distinguishing between users, to fine-grained protection domains.

The most general way of tracking who can access what, and how, in a system, is to use an access matrix. This can be implemented as a global table, capability lists, or access control lists.

▶ Distributed systems are very open to threats to security. There are two aspects to this: mutual authentication of servers and clients and protection of messages passing between them. There is also a need for authentication of machine-readable documents.

FURTHER READING

Fault tolerance in distributed systems is covered by Silberschatz and Galvin Section 16.4; Tanenbaum (1995) Section 4.5. Protection mechanisms are dealt with in Silberschatz and Galvin Chapter 19; Tanenbaum and Woodhull Section 5.5; Tanenbaum (1992) 4.5. For further information on security, see Silberschatz and Galvin Chapter 20; Tanenbaum and Woodhull Section 5.4; Tanenbaum (1992) 4.4; Stallings Chapter 14.

SELF-TEST QUESTIONS

1   Discuss the issues involved in handling faults in a computer system.

> 2 Discuss the mechanisms which could be used to implement security policies in a computer system.
>
> 3 Explain the problem of mutual authentication in a distributed system, and some of the approaches taken.
>
> 4 Outline how secret keys and public keys can be used to encrypt data passing over communication lines.
>
> 5 Explain how digital signatures work.

DISCUSSION QUESTIONS

1 Investigate the procedure known as 'incremental backup'.

2 When a password is typed at the keyboard, even though not echoed on the screen, it is still stored somewhere in memory. Would it be possible to find this part of memory and thus discover another user's password?

3 We have seen that the memory manager implements a reasonably strict protection regime. Would it be possible to make this the basis for all protection in a system?

4 Suggest ways in which the system could enforce protection on two processes performing two-way communication through a shared buffer so that a process has read access only when it should be reading and write access only when it should be writing.

5 If a particular security domain had read access to every object, then a capability list for that domain would have to have an entry for every object. Can you suggest some way of abbreviating this?

6 Suggest a safeguard against attempts to intercept and store messages on a network and replaying them later.

7 Does the use of an authentication server really solve the problem of authentication, or does it just open up the possibility of one really huge hole in security?

8 With reference to the sequence of messages in Figure 8.2, could an imposter masquerade as B and be able to decrypt the message?

9 With public key encryption, how can you be sure that the public key you are using is really that of your intended recipient, and not that of an imposter who intercepts the message and decrypts it?

10 Using the private key to encrypt the document guarantees that only the claimed originator could have encrypted it. But it also means that anyone can read it. Is it possible to have both a digital signature, and an encrypted document?

Reading List

Gray, J. (1997) *Interprocess Communications in Unix*. Upper Saddle River, NJ: Prentice Hall.

Nutt, G. (1997) Operating Systems: a Modern Perspective. Reading, MA: Addison-Wesley.

Rago, S. (1993) Unix System V Network Programming. Reading, MA: Addison-Wesley.

Robbins, K. and Robbins, S. (1996) Practical Unix Programming. Upper Saddle River, NJ: Prentice Hall.

Silberschatz, A. and Galvin, P. (1998) Operating System Concepts, 5th edn. Reading, MA: Addison-Wesley.

Stallings, W. (1995) Operating Systems, 2nd edn. Englewood Cliffs, NJ: Prentice Hall.

Stevens, W. R. (1992) Advanced Programming in the Unix Environment. Reading, MA: Addison-Wesley.

Tanenbaum, A. (1992) Modern Operating Systems. Englewood Cliffs, NJ: Prentice Hall.

Tanenbaum, A. (1995) Distributed Operating Systems. Englewood Cliffs, NJ: Prentice Hall.

Tanenbaum, A. and Woodhull, A. (1997) *Operating Systems: Design and Implementation*, 2nd edn. Upper Saddle River, NJ: Prentice Hall.

Index